SACRED WHISPERS

Sacred Whispers

90 Day Devotional for God's Ears Only

LINDA S. CARTER

A Fresh Wind

Contents

Requests for information should be addressed to
www.LindaSCarter.com

ISBN Number 979-8-988-3639-0-3 *(Paperback)*
ISBN Number 979-8-9883639-1-0 *(Ebook)*

Cover Design: Mia Little / Little Design Studios, Chicago, IL
Interior Design: Marcie Wilson with A Fresh Wind, Lynwood, IL
Publisher: A Fresh Wind, Lynwood, IL
Photo: Chanel Productions Photography & Video Services, Raleigh, NC
Printed in the United States

Sacred Whispers are the most intimate and sacred thoughts and prayers that we reserve for God's ears only.

~ Linda S. Carter

Sacred Whispers
90 Devotionals for God's Ears Only

Inviting God Into Your Sacred Spaces

Linda S. Carter

DEDICATION

To my beloved children, Christopher, Bryan, and Demetria. You inspire me to be what God has declared that I am and that I could have never imagined becoming.

To my husband, Ron, you give meaning to the word and concept of a soulmate, and I love you beyond words.

Introduction

We have all been there. We have all been in the midst of some overwhelming crisis or situation that completely stunned us. By the time we realized how overcome we were by our own emotions, we had lost control of our inhibitions. Inhibitions that kept us from actually saying things that every person in the room would never forget because at that moment we were beyond exasperated. For some, you had this experience in a workplace or a public gathering, or even at an event where you served as a volunteer. For others, you had this experience at a wedding, funeral, family reunion, or other social gathering. Wherever you were in that moment, it was not a *sacred space*.

A *sacred space* is where we can be alone with God. It can be a designated prayer closet, kitchen, office, or bedroom. This is because what makes a space sacred and safe is the presence of God. God is our refuge and intervenes when our inhibitions have fled, and our fear is front and center. Our *sacred spaces* make room for God to be with us and prepare us for every season of our lives. When we invite God into our *sacred spaces,* we are ready to get intimate and personal. It is our intimacy that fortifies our relationship with God. These intimate inter-actions and exchanges with God are what are referred to as *Sacred Whispers* throughout this book.

As you begin to delve into this devotional book, understand that it was written to help its readers and listeners see the value of an intimate relationship with God. Intimate relation-ships are usually reserved for private spaces outside of public view. This is so that intimacy can happen organically and grow and evolve. In the same way, an intimate relationship with God needs a sacred space to develop, grow and evolve. When we are alone with God, and engaged in the process of transparently communicating our thoughts and emotions, then we are creating a *sacred space* for our *sacred whispers.*

Here is what readers and listeners are invited and encouraged to do. First, you are invited to engage God in your own sacred space. Second, you are encouraged to do all of the following at your own pace. Third, you are encouraged to purposely create a safe and intimate space for your *sacred whispers.* Fourth, you are encouraged to create habits and routines for communicating, connecting, and conversing with God. Finally, you are encouraged to disclose and expose all of the issues of your heart to God and do so without any fear of retribution or judgment.

Every devotion presented in this book is an authentic experience. These devotions are intended to guide and assist readers and listeners with the process of release, relinquish, and replenish through sacred whispers. How you engage in this process is your choice, but a tangible *sacred space* has been provided for you to write your *sacred whispers* and insights. Once you have a rhythm to the practice of *sacred whispers,* then you will hopefully begin to embrace a new level of intimacy with God.

There are three sections of this devotional. Each of these sections is to help readers and listeners begin to develop their devotional practices and disciplines. Each devotion has a scripture quotation for reference and reflection. All scripture quotations, unless otherwise noted, are taken from The Holy Bible, New International Version®, NIV®.

Communication. Start at the beginning! These devotions are intended to help you practice the art of *Sacred Whispers* by telling God everything! Of course, God is sovereign and knows, but this does not prevent you from telling God what troubles, frightens, or frustrates you, and saying it in a safe and *sacred space.*

Connection. Stay with it! These devotions are intended to help you with creating a *sacred space* by connecting with God on an intimate level. Remember, *sacred spaces* provide safety. They are a place for you to unpack or process experiences so that you can navigate areas of your life that may be challenging. This is your sacred space, and it is where you meet and connect with God.

Conversation. Schedule the time! The devotions in this section are intended to show you how natural it is to have a conversation with God. A conversation with God does not mean that you talk while God listens. In a conversation, there is a mutual exchange. This means that God talks to you and you in turn talk with God. It is also a time to pause and listen for God's guidance. The only requirement is that you schedule the time for conversations with God. When you have daily conversations with God in a designated sacred space, then you will have the moments needed for reflection, devotion, and prayer.

Finally, remember that God welcomes our communication with Him and is open to being with us every moment. God is watching, even though we have not asked Him to watch over us. God is listening, even though we have not asked Him to listen to us. God is guiding us, even when we have not asked Him for guidance. And God is doing all of this because we are always on God's mind. It doesn't matter where we are in our fellowship with God today, because God welcomes us to come as we are with the issues of our hearts.

As you read or listen to this devotional, remember, that you can create your own *sacred space* for all of your *sacred whispers.*

PART I: COMMUNICATION

COMMUNICATING THROUGH SACRED WHISPER

GOD, FIX ALL OF IT!

In today's devotional moment with God, we talk through the benefits of our transparent prayers. Some of the most intense and intimate prayers, thoughts, or feelings we have ever had were for *God's Ears Only*. God could handle what we choose to conceal from public view because sharing intimate prayer details with those, who by their own proximity, should know our most intimate secrets was not okay or comfortable. This is because our most intimate thoughts were so intense that we could not force ourselves to say them out loud to our spouse, best friend, or pastor. We had convinced ourselves that if we shared, then we would become vulnerable to their judgment, and judgment is something that most of us fear. This is why we have learned to hide behind smiles and stoic faces because it creates a façade of strength. Let's face it, we all want to be labeled as strong, fierce, and courageous.

> "We only need to know when it is time to stop pretending to be strong and start being transparently prayerful."

The truth is that it is easy to become experts at pretending everything is good or fine. The house is a mess, but it's fine.

The overdue bills are piling up, but it's fine. The job is not giving us a desperately needed pay raise, but it's fine. The car is on its last leg, but it's fine. Our marriages or relationships are going through some challenges, but it's fine. Our emotional and physical energy tank is completely empty, but it's fine. And in a moment of breaking, you finally find the sacred space to be transparent enough to prayerfully whisper, *God, fix all of it!*

In these moments of transparency, we find our greatest source of strength, and that is in a sacred space with God. We only need to know when it is time to stop pretending to be strong and start being transparently prayerful.

You are my strength, I sing praise to you; you, God, are my fortress, my God on whom I can rely.

Psalm 59:17

Prayer

Father God, help me to let go of the weight of worry. Help me God to trust you with me, so that I am not overwhelmed by my own existence in a world that is unable to fix what only you can. This is my prayerful whisper. Amen.

Reflection

Invite God into this moment. Experience the calm of letting the weight go. Let God carry you.

What have you been carrying alone for far too long?

Is it time for transparency? What do you need to be transparent about?

What sacred whispers would you like to share with God today?

GOD, TELL ME THE ANSWER TO ALL OF THIS

In today's devotional moment with God, we unpack and talk about candid and honest communication, and how it can foster our relationship with God. If we were to think back to the not-so-distant past, we would probably recall a time in our lives when our relationship with God was a hot mess. This was a time when our prayers were rote, our worship was brief, and our heart was on the fringe of conviction. The problem with life was just living it. Life had hardened us, and our perspective of God was so colored that we couldn't even hear the gospel message. But like most people, we clung to the familiar and kept showing up for church anyhow. Although our neighbors in the pews would try to console and encourage us with, 'God has your answer,' we believed they were pointing us in the right direction but with no instructions to get what we needed.

> "What we have learned from experience is life can migrate from being managed to being messy in minutes. This is why we need to have direct access to God for ourselves."

What we have learned from experience is life can migrate from being managed to being messy in minutes. This is why we need to have direct access to God for ourselves. The prayers of the saints are great, but they cannot speak to the depth of our needs. Our communication needs to be honest conversations that are not sugar-coated and have no omissions that impede our transparency. We cannot hide what is always known to God. This is why we must pursue, petition, and pray until God releases the answers into our lives.

The point of today's devotion is it only takes a moment to reflect back on our past to see how far God has already brought us. Our past has a purpose. It shows us what has been possible because we communicated with God about every-thing, and God released the answers into our lives. When life was at its most challenging points, we prayed, worshiped, gave an offering, and joined in the fellowship of believers. We were doing what was familiar to us. And although we may not have understood it at the time, we had begun to create our line of sacred communication with God.

The past has taught us that life is hard and challenging, but when we stop complaining and start communicating, we can remind ourselves that God can handle what we cannot. Then, in our direct line of sacred communication, prayerfully whisper, God, tell me the answer to all of this.

In the same way, the Spirit helps us in our weakness. We do not know what we ought to pray for, but the Spirit himself intercedes for us through wordless groans.

Romans 8:26

Prayer

Father God, speak to me in the quietness and stillness of this time with you. Let your voice be my compass and my guide so that I will understand how to react to all that is before me. This is my prayerful whisper. Amen.

Reflection

Invite God into this moment. Think about the last time you sat still, quiet, and patiently before God.

What was it that you wanted to say to God?

What did you want God to say to you?

What sacred whispers would you like to share with God today?

GOD, GIVE ME THE GRACE TO NAVIGATE THIS WORLD

In today's devotional moment with God, we talk through why bad things happen to all of us, and why Christians are not exempt. When we were new Christians there was a level of excitement that was unmatched. We had just hit the prover-bial jackpot! We may have even thought that now that we had handed over the guidance of our lives to God, there would be nothing bad that would happen to us or our loved ones. All of the things that we had heard about God were about to pay off. God had us covered and we were in good hands. God heard our prayers and there was going to be an extra layer of protection. God was our new superpower and blanket of protection, and the benefits were going to be abundant. There would be no further encounters with hardships and life would be filled with blessings. The God life would be the best life ever! Sounds amazing, doesn't it? The truth is that God is amazing. The world that we share with billions of people, is not so amazing. This is because there are places in our world where God is not known or accepted and places where He is denied. The level of moral accountability that comes with being a Christian is not the standard for everyone. This means that we will be subject to whatever is conceived in their unbelieving soul.

> "As Christians, we have a purpose, and that is to share the gospel of Jesus Christ through both our witness and words."

The unfortunate part is that we as Christians will not get a free pass that allows us to escape the bad things that may happen. We need to coexist in a world where brutality, cruelty, and tragedy will continue to happen, regardless of our relationship with God. We will continue to meet people who do not share our Christian beliefs, values, or moral compass and have no interest in hearing about the redeeming love of Jesus. As Christians, we have a purpose, and that is to share the gospel of Jesus Christ through both our witness and words. We are destined to live in this world, but we do not have to conform to its norms. What we can do in our sacred spaces is prayerfully whisper, *God, give me the grace to navigate this world.*

Do not conform to the pattern of this world but be transformed by the renewing of your mind. Then you will be able to test and approve what God's will is - His good, pleasing, and perfect will.

Romans 12:2

Prayer

Father God, give me both the courage and an opportunity to speak honestly and boldly about Jesus Christ, and the pricelessness of His redeeming love and compassion. God, strengthen me to navigate this life with your grace. This is my prayerful whisper. Amen.

Reflection

Invite God into this moment. Do you have the courage to share the gospel of Jesus Christ with someone struggling to make sense of this life?

How will you begin the conversation?

What sacred whisper would you like to share with God today?

GOD, DON'T LET ME MISS THIS!

In today's devotional moment with God, we consider the value of communicating effectively with God. So many of the stories in the bible should resonate with us on a more personal level. This is because of the documented interactions between God and mankind. The stories of the bible capture numerous experiences that range from brave and courageous to disappointing and devastating. The question that often surfaces is why people failed to understand the clear instructions they had received from God. But maybe some years from now, when people are reading our memoirs or biographies, they may have similar questions.

One of the best examples of failing to understand God's instruction is found in the story of Adam and Eve. They were told not to eat from one particular tree in the Garden of Eden. God had pointed out the tree by name, compared it to all of the other fruit-bearing trees in the garden, and told them what would happen if they ate its fruit. The one thing that God said that should have caused them to be alarmed was "You shall surely die."

Death is not something that we as humans are comfortable with because it was never meant to be our experience. Adam and Eve had never experienced death and therefore were not familiar with the consequences so clearly defined by God.

They literally missed the point of God's clear directive! Eating the forbidden fruit was going to bring death into their life.

> "Our experiences with God should prompt us to be wiser than our predecessors."

As we reflect on Adam and Eve's story, what should stand out for us is knowing that we can't afford to miss God's instructions for our lives because the consequences can be costly.

Our daily prayer time should include transparent conversations and sacred whispers like *God, please don't let me miss this!* Not only because of the consequences but also because of what we will forfeit. Our experiences with God should prompt us to be wiser than our predecessors. We see by their story what is at stake in our own, especially when we don't pay attention to the details. In obedience, God gives an abundance of blessings and obedience is how we should purpose to live our lives alongside God.

Blessed are all who fear the LORD, who walk in obedience to Him.

Psalm 128:1

Prayer

Father God, help me to always choose obedience in my relationship with you, even when I don't understand your plans for my life. This is my prayerful whisper. Amen.

Reflection

Invite God into this moment. Ask God to help you to always hear and heed His instructions.

What can you teach others about your experiences with being obedient to God?

What sacred whispers would you like to share with God today?

GOD, STRENGTHEN ME TO COPE WITH GODLESS PEOPLE

In today's devotional moment with God, we talk about the spiritual challenges of coping with godless behavior. Most people who we interact with or have interacted with in the past, have by their own experience become a reference of sorts for us. If asked to give a reference to a potential future employer or a volunteer organization, much of their information would be based on what they have observed about us. Their references would include details like whether we came to work on time. Were we organized people who met deadlines or frequently missed key important details for the job? Did we get along well with our colleagues or had a difficult time working with our peers? Although these are good things to know about us, it tells them nothing about our ethics or morals, or identity in Christ Jesus.

Unfortunately, it is easy for people to see what we do, but difficult for people to know who we are. Some of the most organized, people-pleasing, team players have no relationship or belief in the existence of God. Godless people by their very nature have a selfish disposition, and even though they may produce for the employer, they devastate their peers with insult and insolence. Understand that this is not a judgment, but years of personal experience and observation.

> "When we are facing godless people, we must remain steadfast in our faith, and remember that Jesus Christ has already secured the victory."

These experiences with godless people have become far too familiar for many Christians. Christians in the workplace today are continuing to be subjected to the havoc caused by their godless co-workers. The frustrating part is that in most cases, Christians have been prohibited from sharing their faith in the workplace due to state and federal regulations that deem this a form of harassment. In some cases, Christians have questioned whether the devil has been given an edge and won the battle. When we are facing godless people, we must remain steadfast in our faith, and remember that Jesus Christ has already secured the victory. We must never become so frustrated with the situation that we accept that the devil has won out over us. Remember, it only takes a moment to make your requests known and prayerfully whisper, *God, strengthen me to cope with godless people.*

Consider it pure joy, my brothers and sisters, whenever you face trials of many kinds, because you know that the testing of your faith produces perseverance. Let perseverance finish its work so that you may be mature and complete, not lacking anything,

James 1:2-4

Prayer

Father God, help me to stand ready to win souls for Jesus Christ. God, let my Christian witness be a guiding light that leads to you. This is my prayerful whisper. Amen.

Reflection

Invite God into this moment. How will you cope with godless people who challenge your Christian witness?

What will you do to prevent yourself from becoming angry and falling into sin?

What sacred whisper would you like to share with God today?

GOD, PLEASE
DON'T LEAVE ME

In today's devotional moment with God, we talk about how the early influencers of our faith impact our beliefs. Some of us reading or listening to this devotional may recall what it was like to follow the examples set before us in a Christian home. Growing up in a strong Christian family has its pros and cons, and we can probably list several personal experiences that attest to this. When the family is Christian there are moral values that become a part of the family's DNA. These moral values continue to be a part of our spiritual psyche' and are activated most often by some trigger event.

Trigger events can be difficult to navigate, and balancing faith and family with our own fear and frustration can be an even bigger challenge. The truth is that those of us who have been socialized in Christian families would prefer to be seen as faithfully fierce and competent conquerors. Even if this is a stretch of the truth. After all, we have been socialized by our mamas, papas, grandmas, and others to be strong Christians. We have been taught that onlookers and outsiders don't need to know our truth. We are to cover up our fear and pretend to have a grasp of the gospel, even though our grip on that last thread is slipping. Although all of the pretending may work for a while, a landslide of trigger events will cause us to pursue God for ourselves. And when this happens, we begin to make decisions about our relationship with God. We will decide that it didn't matter if our relationship with God didn't mirror our family's standards. And although our heroes and heroines were God-fearing, bible-reading, holy dancing, and praying folks, not once had they said God was the one who had soothed their pains, comforted their souls, knew their truths, and held their secrets. They had learned to go into their prayer closets or sacred spaces and whisper, *God, please don't leave me.* They understood the value of an authentic and intimate relationship with God.

> "These moral values continue to be a part of our spiritual psyche' and are activated most often by some trigger event."

For some of us, it would be many years later before we learned that God had carried our ancestors through the highs and lows of life. Maybe the reason they never mentioned God as their source, was because the real lesson that they wanted us to learn was to pursue God for ourselves.

If any of you lacks wisdom, you should ask God who gives generously to all without finding fault, and it will be given to you.

James 1:5.

Prayer

Father God, help me to continue to pursue my own relationship with you. God, show me how to use my faith-driven experiences to help others. This is my prayerful whisper. Amen.

Reflection

Invite God into this moment. How will you continue to pursue and grow your personal relationship with God?

What lessons from your Christian family still have meaning for you today?

What sacred whisper would you like to share with God today?

GOD, YOU ALONE KNOW MY HEART

In today's devotional moment with God, we talk through the thoughts behind our decision to have a heart for the things of God. What if people could look at you and know your every thought? Would they be surprised to learn that you are not who they thought you were? Would people be shocked to know that your thoughts are not judgments, but are about how to be authentic and faithful to your calling or purpose? Would they be taken aback because your transparency makes you seem less of the gentle Christian that they perceived you to be? Or would they be apologetic for their own preconceived ideas that were based solely on how you appeared through their personal lens? Unfortunately, we have all been guilty of judging people based on how we see them. Our lens has become the standard through which all of our experiences and people are judged as good, bad, or indifferent. Yet, it never occurred to us that it may be time for a vision check to make sure that we are capable of seeing 20/20.

> "Our lens has become the standard through which all of
> our experiences and people are judged as good, bad, or
> indifferent."

Most of the time, if given the opportunity, we would discover that our perceptions are not a reality at all. We would also discover that we lack the supernatural credentials to judge anyone. Personally, there was a period in my life when everything was about the big cover-up. Great effort went into concealing as much as possible. My emotional and mental energy was given to hiding details about myself that would welcome judgment. No one needed to know that I was a struggling single mom working my way through college. No one needed to know that although I presented well because of an extensive vocabulary, my clothes and shoes were second-hand, and my means were meager at best. Even with the little that I had, it was important for me to treat people with dignity, kindness, and respect, and not the bitterness and hurt that I sometimes felt because of hardships. In those moments, I learned compassion and kindness because people judged me based on what they saw, and not who I was. Often, I would prayerfully whisper, *God, you alone know my heart.* I would pray that one day people would see the compassionate and loving soul He had created me to be. Honestly, I believe most of us would want this.

Jesus reminded a group of privileged men who had invited Him to dinner, that the woman who had entered the banquet room uninvited and anointed Him with expensive perfume, would not be remembered for who she was but for what she did. Therefore, let us be mindful that we are to extend God's grace because we are unqualified to judge another human soul.

Truly I tell you, wherever the gospel is preached throughout the world what she has done will also be told, in memory of her."

Mark 14:9

Prayer

Father God, help me to respond to the judgment of others in a way that is God honoring. Let offense not be my response to those who judge me based on what they believe they see, and not the person that you made me to be. This is my prayerful whisper. Amen.

Reflection

Invite God into this moment. What do you think God would want you to say to those who judge you?

What sacred whisper would you like to share with God?

GOD, HELP ME TO LET GO OF MY PAST MISTAKES

In today's devotional moment with God, we talk about the importance of forgiving ourselves. What if we were able to follow our own advice and let it go? What if we told ourselves that today is a good day to let go of our past mistakes but took no action to do it? What if we were able to actually be resolved and decided that the past is the past and moved on? What if we chose to forgive ourselves and had peace about it? The only answer to all of these what-ifs is to respond with definitive action. Let's be honest, looking back at our past mistakes serves no purpose for our spiritual well-being, even though we may try to convince ourselves otherwise. When we hold onto past mistakes that we cannot change or alter or resolve in real time, then we subject ourselves to unnecessary regret. The truth is everyone has some regret about their past mistakes. We may have done some things that wounded people. We may have cost someone their job. We may have caused a marriage to end due to our own behavior. We may have abandoned our children, spouses, family, or friends for our own selfish needs.

Whatever past mistakes we made God has and is willing to forgive us. The only reason we keep replaying past mistakes is because we have not chosen to forgive ourselves. When we find the courage to forgive ourselves, then we will have the personal permission we need to let it go.

> "When we hold onto past mistakes that we cannot change, alter, or resolve in real-time, then we subject ourselves to unnecessary regret."

God keeps no record of right or wrong when we are truly repentant. Although we may be unable to make a definitive decision about our past, God has and did. God's response to our past, present, and future mistakes was Jesus Christ. What we should remember about our past mistakes is that they are over and done with and have already been forgiven. Therefore, forgive that person in the mirror looking back at you and let it go. Then, unbound and unburdened prayerfully whisper, *God, help me to let go of my past mistakes*!

"I, even I, am he who blots out your transgressions, for my own sake, and REMEMBER your sins no more."

Isaiah 43:25

Prayer

Father God, help me to give myself permission to live in the present moments, and not linger in the past. God, let my history be helpful and not hurtful to my future. This is my prayerful whisper. Amen.

Reflection

Invite God into this moment. Ask God to help you with issues of unforgiveness.

What do you need to do to give yourself permission to let go of past mistakes?

What sacred whisper would you like to share with God?

GOD, HELP ME DO BETTER TOMORROW

In today's devotional moment with God, let's talk through our desire to become our better selves. If you have ever awakened in the morning still physically exhausted, mentally tired, and emotionally drained from the previous day's activities, then you will probably be able to relate to this experience. In a personal example, you will understand, hopefully with some level of empathy, when I explain my not-so-good choices. And hopefully, you will not judge me harshly because maybe, just maybe, you have been guilty of the same. There have been mornings when I have felt spiritually imbalanced. What this means is that my interest was diverted to my day instead of my daily routine and time alone with God. I chose to read the world's news instead of the good news of the gospel, and both were available on the same electronic device. I failed to say or pray a single word of thanksgiving to acknowledge God for the blessed life I was living. I realized that I was mentally alert, physically rested, and emotionally calm, but I never once blessed the name of Jesus. I was spiritually imbalanced!

> "Spiritual imbalances happen when our spiritual routine of communicating and connecting with God is disrupted."

Spiritual imbalances happen when our spiritual routine of communicating and connecting with God is disrupted. The disruption is most often caused by the demands of our lives. We are oftentimes so inundated with our daily schedules that we are unaware of our own physical and mental exhaustion, or the unacknowledged stress affecting our spiritual well-being. What we can do is a course correction. This means that we shift, and either begin or end each day with a devotional routine that will keep us spiritually balanced. How we engage God in the morning is important to setting the pace and spiritual tone for the day. How we engage God in the evening creates the space for a restful night. We have to prioritize God in our lives. We have to recognize that being able to finish what we started yesterday, is the gift of God for today.

Like me, maybe you rationalized that God understands and is gracious and loving enough to overlook our spiritual slacking. Although this may be true, spiritual slacking is not okay. We have to be intentional in communicating with God daily. So when a course correction is warranted, prioritize time for God, and prayerfully whisper, *God, help me do better tomorrow.*

But seek first His kingdom and His righteousness, and all these things will be given to you as well. Therefore do not worry about tomorrow, for tomorrow will worry about itself. Each day has enough trouble of its own.

Matthew 6:33-34

Prayer

Father God, help me to define my priorities so they are worthy of my time, energy, and attention. God, guide me so that I am able to sort through the busyness that keeps me from being focused and from being my best self. This is my prayerful whisper. Amen.

Reflection

Invite God into this moment. Ask God to help you do better with managing your priorities.

How will you make God a priority in your life each day?

What sacred whispers would you like to share with God today?

GOD, DON'T LET ANGER CONTROL ME

In today's devotional moment with God, we talk about how we deal with our anger. Anger describes a range of human feelings, thoughts, and emotions. It is probably safe to say that everyone has experienced anger at some point in their life. We may have become angry because of an unanticipated situation, or due to a disagreement, or disrespectful behavior towards us. Whatever the cause of our angered response, the situation probably caught us off guard. But our response to anger matters. It matters because if left unchecked it can cause physical, mental, and spiritual harm.

Candidly, most people are not looking for a fight or reason to be angry. We are content with as little chaos and conflict as possible. We will apply a great deal of self-control and restraint to avoid people with strong opposing opinions that may cause us to react with anger. We are even cautious about being with people groups in places where we may need to defend ourselves because of possible character assassination. Although some may call this avoidant behavior, we define our behavior as discerning. When we know that certain people or situations can trigger angry emotions, then we must follow Jesus' example and turn away from it. This is because as followers of Jesus, people are always watching us to see how we will respond when conditions turn unfavorable. While people are watching our witness let us choose to be imitators of Jesus, so that no one will label us an imposter of the faith.

> "When we know that certain people or situations can trigger angry emotions, then we must follow Jesus' example and turn away from it."

We may be surprised to hear that anger is not the problem. Learning to control our anger so that we can let offenses go is the real challenge. Whenever we feel triggered to respond with anger, we must remember who we are in the family of God. We must quickly forgive the offense and the offender because forgiveness is an expectation of God and benefits our well-being. We should always look to God for opportunities to resolve any residual angst. This is why we really need our sacred spaces. A safe space allows us to process our anger so that we don't act out our anger. God is listening, and when we are struggling with issues of anger, we should turn to Him and prayerfully whisper, *God, don't let anger control me.*

"In your anger do not sin": Do Not Let the sun go down while you are still angry, and do not give the devil a foothold.

Ephesians 4:26-27

Prayer

Father God, help me to manage my anger so that it does not consume me, and cause me harm. This is my prayerful whisper. Amen.

Reflection

Invite God into this moment. Ask God to help you to let go of the anger that you feel toward others.

How has unresolved anger affected your life?

How will you be intentional in processing your anger issues with God?

What sacred whisper would you like to share with God?

GOD, GIVE ME THE COURAGE TO SPEAK OUT

In today's devotional moment with God, we talk about having the courage to stand up for what is right. Many of us remember being a child who played with the neighborhood kids on the block. The rules for these childhood games were often subject to interpretation. Like most subjective matters, there was plenty of room and opportunity to adjust the rules, depending on which team was winning or losing the game. As children, we would often change the rules to give our team a winning edge. This is because we were children. Children, who by their age and experience were only able to reason from an immature intellect. Children, who never thought they were cheating. Children, who never considered losing friends because they couldn't be trusted to play fair. Children, who laughed and teased their opponents as they tried to figure it out. Our friends had questioned us back in those days. They had wondered if we could change the rules, and although we knew it wasn't fair, it was just for fun. Regardless of whichever team you were on, we knew we would play together again without grudges or hurt feelings because it was just child's play.

> "This is the reason no Christian should be comfortable with being a bystander when Jesus Christ has called us to be advocates for the powerless and voiceless."

As mature adults, we would be hard-pressed to tolerate an employer, colleague, peer, or friend who changes the rules of engagement. Especially when we are rising in our careers and winning in our life circumstances. As adults, we have to be responsible with how we handle people. All people have value and matter to God. This truth is the reason we should be consciously moral with our actions. It is the reason we should have the integrity to be fair with everyone at every opportunity.

The point is that we are no longer children making up the rules as we go because we understand that people's lives will be impacted. This is the reason no Christian should ever be comfortable with being a bystander when Jesus Christ has called us to be advocates for the powerless and voiceless. This is why we need to pray for the courage to stand up for what is right, just, and fair. Then, when we retreat to our sacred spaces to pray, we will be confident in our prayerful whisper, *God, give me the courage to speak out.*

Then you will understand what is right and just and fair—every good path. For wisdom will enter your heart, and knowledge will be pleasant to your soul.

Proverbs 2:9-10

Prayer

Father God, give me fearless faith to stand firmly as an advocate for justice, truth, and righteousness. This is my prayerful whisper. Amen.

Reflection

Invite God into this moment. Ask God to help you be courageous in your faith, and to take a stand against what is unfair and unjust towards all people.

As a Christian, how can you make a difference and be an advocate for all people?

What sacred whisper would you like to share with God today?

GOD, NOTHING IS TOO HARD FOR YOU

In today's devotional moment with God, we talk about the meaning of God's omnipotence in our lives. God is never surprised. God knows the time the sun will rise, and the time the sun will set into the horizon. God knows when the seasons will change, the rain will fall, the time of the morning the birds will sing, and the bees will buzz once more. God knows your thoughts and your dreams, the number of days you will live, and the very day your life will become immortal. And although the most brilliant scientists on the earth were surprised by the Novel Coronavirus known as COVID-19, God was not. God knew exactly how humanity would respond to this global pandemic, and how it would devastate populations around the world. God has never been and will never be surprised by anything that has happened, is happening, and will happen in all of creation. This is because God is the Sovereign Creator of the heavens and earth and all that is tangible and intangible.

> "God has never been and will never be surprised by anything that has happened, is happening, and will happen in all of creation."

For some, the faith-driven fact that God is never surprised, and commands creation will be a challenging concept to grasp. This may be because they are not convicted or convinced by the message of the Bible which speaks to the deity, sovereignty, and holiness of God. Understand that for Christians, it is the reason we can face each day with hope. Whether the stock market rises or falls, God's provisions will remain the same. When an existential crisis like we have faced with COVID-19 has come and gone, God will prove to be faithful. When the world's powers and leaders stand powerless and lost for solutions, God's power will make a path forward for peace and balance. When we are uncertain about our future, God knows the plan for our prosperity. When we are overcome with life because we cannot figure out what to do, we have learned that our prayerful whisper, *God nothing is too hard for you,* will not fall on deaf ears. Today, let this devotional moment which echoes God's omnipotence provide us with hope in uncertain times. Let our hope in God, and our faith in the promises of Jesus, guide us in a world that is continually changing.

Know therefore that the Lord your God is God; He is the faithful God, keeping his covenant of love to a thousand generations of those who love him and keep his commandments.

Deuteronomy 7:9

Prayer

Father God, teach me to genuinely trust you with my life, and the lives of those I love. God, let your Spirit gently nudge me as a reminder of who you are to your creation. This is my prayerful whisper. Amen.

Reflections

Invite God into this moment. Ask God to give you resilient faith.

How have you trusted God with your life during the difficult seasons?

What guidance can you give to others about trusting God with their life?

What sacred whispers would you like to share with God today?

GOD, PLEASE

In today's devotional moment with God, we talk about the importance of being reverent and humble towards God. As a personal reflection, I remember some years ago sitting in a small church in rural South Georgia. It was a bright, sunny, and extremely warm summer day. The front door to the church was propped open for people to enter the building easily, but also as a sign of welcome. The central air in the building was blowing hard to cool the space, but because it was so hot outside it made the sanctuary humid and sticky. As the church began to fill, I noticed the children first. They were dressed in their best Sunday attire. Before their parents could get seated, they were already fidgeting in their seats. In front of the church were two pews filled with about a dozen women. All were dressed in white dresses or skirts and suits and wore the most beautifully adorned hats I had ever seen. They were not just noticeable because of the coordinated clothing, but because of how they fanned the air frantically to find some relief from the warmth of the building. Across the aisle, was a pew of six deacons who were dressed in suits, heavy starched button-down shirts with neckties, and carefully polished shoes. Just as my family took our seats, one of the deacons moved to the microphone standing in the front center aisle. In an attention-grabbing moment, the elderly thin tall man took the microphone from its holder, went down on his knees, and began the most beautiful call to worship I had heard in a very long time. The prayer was simple, specific, and a deliberate petition to God on behalf of all of the souls in and outside of the sanctuary. He began each of the petitions with these two words: *God, please.*

> "God is our Sovereign Lord, and there is no other comparable to Him in all the earth."

There have been many times when I have earnestly prayed to God. My prayers were sincere and filled with the humility of a person who recognized themselves as being a created soul. But there have been other times in my life when struggles and hardships were too much, and instead of asking God for divine intervention, I demanded that it be given immediately.

Regardless of our situations, whether we are in crisis or celebration, there should never be a time when we feel entitled to approach God with anything other than a humble and reverent posture. God is our Sovereign Lord, and there is no other comparable to Him in all the earth. With this truth in our hearts and minds, we should never forget that God is to be worshiped and praised.

"How Great you are, sovereign LORD! There is no one like you, and there is no GOD but you, as we have heard with our ears.

2 Samuel 7:22

Prayer

Father God, help me to always be mindful of your holiness. God, let me always approach you with humility and reverence so that my soul will be anchored in you. This is my prayerful whisper. Amen.

Reflection

Invite God into this moment. Ask the Holy Spirit to guide you and teach you how to speak with God with humility and reverence.

How can you be more open to the presence of holiness in your daily journey?

What sacred whispers would you like to share with God today?

GOD, THANK YOU FOR THE YES

In today's devotional moment with God, we talk through the blessing of a *yes* answer from God. Has it ever occurred to us that prayer isn't something we have to do? Do we pray because we have been taught that it is what makes us a good person? Or do we pray because we want God to act on our endless wish list that we believe will make this life better? Whatever our reasons are for praying, be mindful that there is seldom a time when we go into the presence of God without a full-fledged agenda or a list of specific petitions. Whether our prayer life is the result of learned behaviors, traditions passed down through the generations, or a ritual practice of our faith, our prayer life has a purpose. The purpose of prayer is to make our petitions known to God because we are praying for the desires of our hearts.

We know that when we pray, God can turn our prayer into blessings. However, this does not mean that every agenda or petition prayed will be given an unequivocal *yes* answer. As upsetting as a no answer has been for us at times in our lives, we realize now that the no answers were equally as important as all of the yeses. If we were to honestly reflect on some of the petitions we made to God, then we would agree that God's no answer was the right answer. This is because in hindsight we can clearly see that God was protecting us. We were in jeopardy of making a mistake or error that could have resulted in long-term consequences for our lives, but God would not give us the green light, and this was a saving grace.

> "As upsetting as a no answer has been for us at times in our lives, we realize now that the no answers were equally as important as all of the yeses."

In prayer, we can talk with God about every worry, anxiety, or concern of our hearts without any judgment. In prayer, we can talk with God about our singleness, marriages, and family dynamics without criticism. In prayer, we can receive revelation and understand that every no answer was given to us because it was not our season or for our benefit. In prayer we can talk with God intimately and prayerfully whisper, *God thank you for the yes.*

The takeaway from today's devotional is that prayer life is a privileged life. Therefore, when we go to God in our sacred spaces, remember, that He weighs our agendas and petitions and answers with what is best for us.

Do not be anxious about anything, but in every situation, by prayer and petition, with thanksgiving, present your requests to God. And the peace of God, which transcends all understanding, will guard your hearts and your minds in Christ Jesus.

Philippians 4:6-7

Prayer

Father God, thank you for the no answers that kept me from going down the wrong path. God, may I always seek your wisdom and guidance through my prayer life. This is my prayerful whisper. Amen.

Reflection

Invite God into this moment. How will you handle the *no* seasons in your life?

What will you do to faithfully follow God's leading and wait for the *yes* answer?

What sacred whisper would you like to share with God today?

GOD, LET ME LIVE THE FAITHFUL LIFE

In today's devotional moment with God, we talk through the reason we should desire to live a faithful life in the presence of God. Normally when we think about our relationship with God, we immediately think about the benefits and blessings that will be afforded to us throughout our lifetime. We become laser-focused on being our best selves by walking the walk and talking the talk of a Christian. We will do everything we can to live life as close to perfect as an imperfect person can. But rarely if ever, do we consider the expectations God has for us as a part of our mutual relationship with Him. We may not be aware of it, but God has expectations for us, just like we have expectations for God. Unfortunately, so many of our expectations have been for things that provide temporary happiness.

Although we may achieve some memorable successes, they will have no importance to our future self. No one will remember that we were once a popular high school cheerleader. No one will remember that we led our college football team to the state championship. No one will remember that we once appeared on the local news as a community advocate who organized an effort to support the safety of our city's neighborhoods. No one will remember, because these efforts although noble, had no lasting benefit for other people in our world.

What we will be remembered for is living out the expectation of God to expose souls to Jesus Christ. This means that when we introduce people to Jesus and they invite Him into their lives, God will meet their needs with unimaginable resources, and He will receive the glory and honor.

> "What we will be remembered for is living out the expectation of God to expose souls to Jesus Christ."

What God has given to all of us in Jesus Christ has exceeded any expectations we could have had for Him. In Jesus Christ, we have received from God the promise of salvation, eternal life, and the gift of the Holy Spirit. These promises are active and everlasting. Jesus Christ demonstrated in His brief but salvific life, that there are innumerable benefits to living a faithful life to God. Therefore, when we go into our sacred space and begin to process our mutual expectations, let our prayerful whisper be, *God, let me live a faithful life.*

No matter how many promises God has made, they are "Yes" in Christ. And so, through Him, the "Amen" is spoken by us to the glory of God.

1 Corinthians 1:20

Prayer

Father God, help me to engage each day with purposeful expectation and with faith. This is my prayerful whisper. Amen.

Reflection

Invite God into this moment. Ask God what a faithful life might look like for you.

What will you do daily to be an example of a life that honors and gives glory to God?

What sacred whispers would you like to share with God today?

GOD, LET MY LIFE HONOR YOU

In today's devotional moment with God, we talk through the many interpretations of success. A common goal among today's readers or listeners is the desire to achieve personal and professional success. For some, success is the achievement of name recognition and facial notoriety. For others, success means an elevation in social class and access to hierarchies and institutions previously inaccessible. However, the definition of success has become broader by societal standards and has taken on new meaning. Success is no longer solely synonymous with people whose discoveries, ideologies, or inventions shifted cultural standards, cured diseases, or even brokered peace. Success as a broader and evolved definition is now attributed to social media influencers or viral videos and virtual movements. If that isn't surprising enough, success is also attributed to creators of bestselling bizarre products, unconventional groups for outrageous or unpopular platforms, or individuals generating media content that appeals to some particular segment of the culture. The profound truth about earthly success is that it is not transcendent. This means that the fame, fortune, and perceived power that some people will experience will not go beyond their lives on earth. In time, their successes will fade from societal memory. However, God who is the true source of success, will always remember the life we have lived.

> "His earthly life and His success were not just measured by faithful obedience, but by how He honored God with His life."

History has shown us that those who were once at the upper echelons of their respective social, political, religious, and philanthropic institutions have long been forgotten for their significant contributions to their societies. Today their successes are not being reported routinely. There are no paparazzi following archaeological expeditions for a footprint of their past life. No one is tweeting or texting or sharing their stories on social media. However, there is one who is an exception. This exception is the life and legacy of Jesus Christ. His life continues to be relevant to us today. Jesus still has a dominant presence on social media, and there are archaeological expeditions dedicated to reconstructing his life's journey. Jesus was pursued by many in His lifetime on earth and is continuing to be pursued by many today. Jesus' fame, miraculous power, and riches in glory have all transcended His earthly life. His success was not just measured by faithful obedience, but by how He honored God with His life. So let us follow His lead and in our sacred spaces prayerfully whisper, *God, let my life honor you.*

Command those who are rich in this present world not to be arrogant nor to put their hope in wealth, which is so uncertain, but to put their hope in God, who richly provides us with every-thing for our enjoyment.

1 Timothy 6:17

Prayer

Father God, teach me to be a beacon for Jesus Christ by my words, actions, and deeds. Let my life lived before you be my truest measure of success. This is my prayerful whisper. Amen.

Reflection

Invite God into this moment. How will you redefine the meaning of success?

What does a successful life that pleases God look like for you?

What sacred whisper would you like to share with God today?

GOD, HELP ME TO SEE YOUR PLANS

In today's devotional moment with God, we talk about the importance of having God's plan right in front of us at all times. In this devotional moment of personal reflection, I can recall being a new high school graduate with some pretty big ambitions. The plan was to land a starting secretarial assistant position in one of the major corporations in my hometown. In those days it was not unheard of to begin a career without a college degree. Like so many other inner-city kids, the plan was to transition into the professional workforce as a secretary. I had decided that the armed services, meat packing job, or local grocer were not a good fit. Even though there was nothing wrong with these jobs, my ambition was to land a corporate secretarial position with paid vacations, insurance benefits, and a retirement pension. As idealistic as this sounds with a high school diploma, my ambition was not. Some people had attested to being a high school graduates who had worked their way up the corporate ladder. They had shared their stories with classes of impressionable high school students and described how their commitment to working hard had resulted in the management positions they held. These corporate executives had boasted to ambitious teenagers that their accomplishments happened with only a high school diploma. The central message was to encourage students to stay in school, graduate and then come and work for their companies. Although the corporate representatives intended to encourage students, it took only a few rejection letters to understand that corporations hire experienced applicants and not recent high school graduates. The unfortunate lesson was that these corporate executives and managers had not been completely transparent either due to a lack of knowledge or a lack of concern.

> "God knows our future and has a plan for it. God has invested significantly in us with the sacrifice of His Son Jesus."

As we reflect on our younger ambitious selves, we should remember that progress toward our personal goals and ambitions took time. In that period, we gained wisdom, knowledge, understanding, and experience. What we may not have understood then was that our future was not in the hands of any corporation or executive. But time allowed us to grow. This growth included the development of our faith. With understanding, we recognized that God had designed a purposeful plan for our lives. Mentors, role models, and motivational speakers had no such plan for us. Their role in that moment of presentation was to simply inspire students to graduate. They had no foreknowledge of our future, and no investment in our success. God knows our future and has a plan for it. God has invested significantly in us with the sacrifice of His Son Jesus. God's plan is to give us purpose to prosper, hope to anticipate the harvest, and the peace that assures us that we are protected. In essence, God has our lives all planned. This is why we should check with God first before we proceed with any planning for our future. Then, with a grateful heart prayerfully whisper, *God, help me to see your plans.*

For I know the plans I have for you," declares the Lord, "plans to prosper you and not to harm you, plans to give you hope and a future.

Jeremiah 29:11

Prayer

Father God, help me to seek you concerning the plans that you have for my life, so it may be lived to your glory. This is my prayerful whisper. Amen.

Reflection

Invite God into this moment. Ask God to show you how to live according to His plans for you.

What do you desire and believe is a part of God's plan for your life that you may not have received yet?

What will you do to make the necessary adjustments to fully align your plans with God's plan?

What sacred whisper would you like to share with God today?

GOD, PLEASE SHOW UP AND SHOW OUT

In today's devotional moment with God, we talk through some childhood experiences and our understanding of God in those moments. As we revisit some of our upbringing as children, there are probably childhood memories that bring a smile to our face. This is because some of those memories are sweet and funny, while others were downright mischievous and precocious. When we recall most of our childhood memories, we will usually remember the response of our parents. In hindsight, our parents were probably mortified by some of the things we said and did.

For the older generations of readers and listeners, your parents were probably like mine and were very formal in their social interactions. A lot of their formal behaviors were probably instilled in you. Formal behaviors meant there were governing rules. Our parents gave us the full list of appropriate behaviors for home, school, church, and public outings. Their list was short but absolute and was the standard to be followed at all times. You were never to say or do anything that embarrassed your parents or yourselves. You were never to address any adult by anything other than the titles by which they had been introduced. You were never to answer an adult's question without placing the words *ma'am, sir, Mr., or Miss* either before or after your response. And the most important rule of these rules is you were never to 'show out'. Showing out meant you expressed disagreement about a decision your parents made, and thereby were disobedient. According to your parent's handbook of rules, the 'no' was never to be questioned, and the 'yes' was a gift of grace. Breaking any of your parent's rules meant that there was going to be a consequence. Consequences ranged from a spanking to having all of your very limited privileges revoked, and whenever your parents had to whisper, '*Stop showing out*', you knew for certain that you were in trouble for not following your social conditioning. The goal of your parents' rules was to raise children who were obedient, socially conscious, and respectful.

> "When God divinely intervenes, challenges are transformed into opportunities, burdens have the potential to produce benefits, and blessings CAN be traced over a lifetime."

In today's Christian culture, the phrase 'showing out' has taken on a whole different meaning. It is no longer a warning given to us by our parents to indicate that we have broken their rules, but it's a reference to the supernatural intervention of God. Our prayerful whisper, *God, please show up and show out*, is a call for God to do something supernaturally amazing. When God divinely intervenes, challenges are transformed into opportunities, burdens have the potential to produce benefits, and blessings cannot be traced over a lifetime. This is the benefit of being a benefactor of the promise given to us through Jesus Christ. Although the social conditioning of our parents was intended to curtail our mischief, let us take from this the respect, honor, and reverence we should render to God, who produces divine interventions that bless, protect, and preserve His children.

No discipline seems pleasant at the time, but painful. Later on, however, it produces a harvest of righteousness and peace for those who have been trained by it.

Hebrews 12:11

Prayer

Father God, help me to live in obedience and always be reverent towards you. God, I believe that when I call out to you, you are there, and will produce divine interventions that are for my good. God, continue to preserve, prosper, and protect me. This is my prayerful whisper. Amen.

Reflection

Invite God into this moment. What is happening today in your life that you need God to show up and show out?

What sacred whispers would you like to share with God today?

GOD, KEEP THE NEGATIVE OUT OF MY LIFE

In today's devotional moment with God, we talk about keeping negative influences out of our lives. Would you be surprised to learn that there are people who are drawn to negativity? As puzzling as this sounds, the negative stuff seems to excite some people. This group of people seem to view others' misfortunes as an unfolding drama. Their interest is beyond normal concern. This is because their interest in another person's misfortunate has nothing to do with concern. Their goal is to gossip. People gossip for several reasons, and avoiding their issues is one of them. A useful tool for handling negative people and their gossip is to withdraw opportunities for them to spread rumors. What if we took personal responsibility for allowing people to gossip to us and acknowledged it is unacceptable? What if we responded differently to the familiar gossipers in our lives and called attention to their inappropriate behavior? What if the next time a gossiper called to tell us about someone else's misfortune, we cut them off in mid-sentence and suggested a moment of prayer for that person's situation?

> "When we are spiritually discerning, we weigh every word."

Every time we listen to gossip and negative comments about someone else, we assume equal responsibility for the harm it can potentially cause. We may attempt to justify listening, but listening gave the gossiper the green light to continue. This is the reason it is important to be spiritually discerning. When we are spiritually discerning, we weigh every word. This helps us to avoid the snare of the devil and revel in another soul's misfortune. We have to be consciously aware of guarding our hearts and minds by admonishing gossipers for their ill-willed behavior. We should never allow anyone to share gossip meant to discourage or harm another soul. Instead, we must use our time wisely in our sacred spaces, and prayerfully whisper, *God, keep the negative out of my life.*

Do not let any unwholesome talk come out of your mouths, but only what helps build others up according to their needs, that it may benefit those who listen.

Ephesians 4:29

Prayer

Father God, help me to be intentional in handling what is shared with me carefully and confidentially, and to not be given into the negativity of gossip. This is my prayerful whisper. Amen.

Reflection

Invite God into this moment. Ask God for direction in handling the gossipers and promoters of negative behaviors in your life, especially those who are closest to you.

How will you influence others to turn away from negativity that is harmful?

What sacred whisper would you like to share with God today?

GOD, YOU ARE WITH ME

In today's devotional moment with God, we talk about what it means to be spiritually aware of God's presence with us. One of the affirming truths we have about God is that He is omnipresent, and a part of our daily experience. Knowing God is with us is what gives us the courage to navigate each day. Spiritually, God is home and our dwelling place. Physically, home is where we live and find refuge and safety. Not because of alarms or locks but because of the presence of God. In our homes behind closed doors is where we usually experience some of the most deeply personal, intimate, and intensely private moments of our lives. This is why our homes are perfect places for our sacred spaces with God. It is also why our homes serve as a beacon to remind us that God is with us.

In personal reflection, as a Chaplain I had the privilege of listening to people's stories. Some of these stories were beautiful experiences and some were sad. Some of the stories defied reasonable explanations and can only be described as miracles. Although people's stories were vastly different in experience, there was a common thread. All of the people shared that after enduring some unforeseen crises and situations, they had survived and were able to return to their homes safely. Each of their stories detailed what happened all around them, but never happened to them. One person recalled being involved in a multi-car collision but miraculously survived the pile-up. Another person recalled how a tornado had swept through their community, and their home was only one of a few that had not been reduced to a pile of rubble. Another person remembered a family member who had suffered a major health incident, but fully recovered and was able to continue to live alone in their own home. In fact, all of their stories had a happy ending and worked out for their own good. God was with them from the time they left home, until the time they returned home.

> "Sometimes just knowing that God is with us is more than enough."

When we whisper prayers to God in our sacred spaces it's not always for the purpose of having a divine intervention. Sometimes just knowing that God is with us is more than enough. There is a comfort that comes with trusting God to be present in our lives and knowing that He is present because we have a relationship.

Our physical homes are not our truest refuge. God is our shelter and dwelling place. Before we begin or end the day, let us take a moment to prayerfully whisper, *God you are with me.*

Whoever dwells in the shelter of the Most High will rest in the shadow of the Almighty. I will say of the Lord, "He is my refuge and my fortress, my God, in whom I trust."

Psalm 91:1-2

Prayer

Father God, help me to always place my faith, hope, and trust in you. God, you alone are my shelter and my refuge, and for this, I praise and thank you. This is my prayerful whisper. Amen.

Reflection

Invite God into this moment. Ask God to help you trust Him.

What miraculous experiences have you had that helped you to know that God was with you?

How can you encourage others to do the same?

What sacred whisper would you like to share with God today?

GOD, HELP ME MANAGE MY PRIDE

In today's devotional moment with God, we talk about the need to be consciously careful with our words. The caution is to never say what we really don't mean. Our words have power. All of us have probably had an intense moment of frustration. We spoke out loud harsh words that were indicative of an emotional moment instead of an experience with a person. We really didn't mean it. Not only did we say harsh words, but we said it in the presence of other people and those words can't ever be retracted or forgotten. Whether you have been on the giving or receiving end of harsh words, it is never a pleasant experience.

> "Take heed to think before you speak, and pray before you act pridefully towards others because there is no way to reverse the harm caused by harsh words."

If you have ever had the experience of speaking without thinking, then you will probably relate to the familiar experience of seeing someone's facial expression after you have grossly misspoken. In these moments our moral compass should trigger feelings of unease and regret. This is because we understand that regardless of how many times we will apologize in the future, 'sorry' and 'please forgive me', will never seem like enough. Even when a great deal of time has passed, people will never forget how we made them feel. And possibly unbeknownst to us there are people who have been on the receiving end of our words, who have vowed to never cross our path in the future. This is why we should be mindful of not just our words but of our temperament. By controlling our emotions we can have greater control of our words.

Experience has shown us that behind brazen words are thoughts and feelings of pride and entitlement. If your position, education, experience, or age, has led you to believe that you can say whatever you think, then you would be correct. The truth is you can, but with your status comes even greater responsibility. It is the responsibility that requires you to be emotionally and spiritually mature enough to handle the privilege without being prideful. This is the reason we should retreat to our sacred spaces and ponder whether pride, anger, or other issues are provoking emotions and words that are potentially harmful. Whatever we discover, remember a prayerful whisper of, *God, help me manage my pride*, can make a difference. Therefore, take heed to think before you speak, and pray before you act pridefully toward others because there is no way to reverse the harm caused by harsh words.

The tongue has the power of life and death, and those who love it will eat its fruit.

Proverbs 18:21

Prayer

Father God, help me to overcome pride that is spiritually blinding so that I may be who you have created me to be. This is my prayerful whisper. Amen.

Reflection

Invite God into this moment. Ask God to help you recognize and address pride and entitlement in your life.

How has your pride affected you in the past?

What will you do to make sure that you are not being influenced by prideful behavior?

What sacred whisper would you like to share with God today?

GOD, HELP ME WITH MY BITTERNESS AND BOUNDARIES

In today's devotional moment with God, we talk about the importance of personal boundaries and how they are useful for self-care and preventing bitterness. Have you ever wondered if Jesus Christ felt neglected by those who were a part of His inner circle? Has it ever even occurred to us that Jesus' constant companions were also His responsibility? Jesus bore the weight of provider, protector, and peace giver but was able to successfully balance boundaries and self-care and His example continues to be relevant to us today.

Many of us have struggled with balancing our priorities. By our own choice, we were the person who made sure everyone's needs were met but neglected our own. The result of self-neglect was physical fatigue, emotional exhaustion, and spiritual depletion. Then, when we had nothing left to give, we became frustrated, angry, and bitter. In Jesus' example, we read how He ministered to the masses and met all of their physical, mental, and spiritual needs. Jesus was both human and divine and it made sense that He would be the designated go-to guy. If someone needed healing, food, shelter, or even forgiveness then Jesus was the one who could handle it. The issue is that while we might be the go-to person for family, friends, and neighbors we have no supernatural abilities to calm the storms in their lives, heal their wounds, provide for their needs, or answer their prayers. We may feel like a superhuman for caring and helping but we still have only a natural ability.

> "Jesus knew the value of having a sacred space where He could be alone with God and used it as often as He needed."

How is it that while taking care of everybody else's needs Jesus never became bitter? Is it because Jesus recognized when it was time to take a break and rest? Jesus knew the value of having a sacred space where He could be alone with God and used it as often as He needed. The problem we have is that we are responsible for the neglect we feel. We are addicted to helping. We ignore the boundaries that God has given us to balance our well-being. We have become so focused on helping that the words yes and no are no longer a part of our vocabulary. Neglect happens because we fail to adhere to self-care boundaries that would allow us to have the much-needed time to rest. At the root of the issue is our need to be the savior and solution for everyone. The hard truth is people don't need a savior when they already have one in Jesus. It's time to re-evaluate our boundaries and stop being bitter with people who are unaware of the unspoken expectations we have for them. Start with self-care first, and if more is needed, ask God. This is why we need to have the safety of our sacred spaces to pray and communicate with God. Once we understand our own needs, we can prayerfully whisper, *God, help me with bitterness and boundaries.*

Cast all your anxiety on him because he cares for you.

1 Peter 5:7

Prayer

Father God, help me to understand and apply boundaries to my life so that no root of bitterness can grow. This is my prayerful whisper. Amen.

Reflection

Invite God into this moment. What will you do to create healthy boundaries for your own self-care?

What will you do with the intention to ensure that you prevent bitterness from becoming an issue in your life?

What sacred whispers do you want to share with God today?

GOD, HELP ME BE BETTER

In today's devotional moment with God, we talk about how to be better in our relationship with God and others. To say that relationships are hard work is probably an understatement. Relationships are filled with so many expectations. Although some of these expectations are spoken, most are not. There is an expectation that we compromise and sacrifice in our relationships, regardless of whether this will be mutual. There is an expectation that we invest time, energy, and attention in our relationship, but with no expectation of being appreciated for it. There is an expectation that we forgive and forget transgressions that have caused sorrow so significant, that the memory of the incident makes us hurt all over again. These expectations beg the question, why in the world would anyone want to be in a relationship? The answer is that God created us to be relational.

God's intention in creation was not only that we be in a relationship with Him, but that we desire to be in a relationship with each other. God intends that we be a partner in a relationship that is mutually loving and forgiving. Unfortunately, somewhere along the way we began to think about our own needs, our own survival, our own success, and our own happiness. The human relationship suffered because we wanted more for ourselves than we did for those we professed to care about and love.

> "God's intention in creation was not only that we ARE in a relationship with Him, but that we desire to be in a relationship with each other."

Although selfish ambition is a contributing factor, it is not the only reason relationships are being targeted and attacked. The devil most surely has a stake in the destruction of anything that God has created and declared as good. Until we begin to change our hearts and minds about how God intended for us to co-exist, we will continue to push for success and autonomy instead of lasting relationships.

God wants us to experience the companionship of another soul that reasons, chooses, feels, and loves. Today, let us identify the disconnects in our relationships and make a conscious effort to reconnect with the people we love and value. In our sacred spaces, let us communicate with God about where we have fallen short, and what we need to do to be reconciled in these relationships. Then ask in a prayerful whisper, *God, help me be better.*

Do nothing out of selfish ambition or vain conceit. Rather, in humility value others above yourselves, not looking to your interests but each of you to the interests of the others.

Philippians 2:3-4

Prayer

Father God, help me to embrace relationships that are for my good and my growth. This is my prayerful whisper. Amen.

Reflection

Invite God into this moment. Ask God to help you figure out who you have become disconnected from in your relationships.

What benefit will you bring to your relationships to further their growth and your own?

What sacred whisper would you like to share with God today?

GOD, GIVE ME SPIRITUAL CLARITY

In today's devotional moment with God, we talk about the benefit of spiritual clarity. Spiritual clarity will help us to stop stressing and praying at the same time. This may seem like a strange statement to make, but it has become an increasingly common practice for people of faith. We are faithful in our walk with God and are committed to praying daily when no woes or worries are troubling us. However, when things are not working in our favor, our daily prayers turn to urgent petitions. It is with this urgency that we ask God for help to cure our situations and calm our troubled souls. But within minutes of saying amen, as an affirmation that we trust and believe God, we move swiftly into planning a solution that may or may not be successful. Behind the stress is this need for an immediate response to our prayers from God. The unfortunate truth is God's timing does not necessarily align with our own urgency. Still, timing is not the only issue. How God answers our prayers, and how they are manifested, can also be an issue. This is because we have imagined what our answered prayers should look like, and if it's different than we have anticipated, then it can be hard to reconcile that it's actually God's answer to our request. The failure to recognize God's answer may also be the reason some believers think that their prayers have gone unanswered.

> "Spiritual clarity helps us with our spiritual lens so that we are capable of seeing God's supernatural response to our lives."

Instead of being frustrated with God, we need to prayerfully whisper, *God give me spiritual clarity*. Spiritual clarity helps us with our spiritual lens so that we are capable of seeing God's supernatural response to our lives. When we can recognize God in our human experience, then our faith grows, and our capacity to be effective as an advocate of Christ Jesus is enhanced. Therefore, we need to stop stressing and start believing that our prayers are in process and God is unquestionably faithful.

Let us hold unswervingly to the hope we profess, for he who promised is faithful.

Hebrews 10:23

Prayer

Father God, give me patience and spiritual clarity to embrace what you have for me in my unanswered prayers. This is my prayerful whisper. Amen.

Reflection

Invite God into this moment. What can you do to be more spiritually aware of God's answers to your prayers?

How does your impatience affect your spiritual lens?

What sacred whisper would you like to share with God today?

GOD, GIVE ME THE RIGHT SPIRIT

In today's devotional moment with God, we talk through the reason we should be mindful of our humility. Do we understand the meaning of humility? Most of us would say that we do and may even argue that we are intentional in our efforts to be as humble as possible. This is because humility is important for Christians. Humility is such a big deal among Christians that we have even gone as far as to decline accolades for our achievements and accomplishments. Although all of this is well-meaning, none of it authentically resembles the selflessness we should embody as the truest definition of humility. Realistically, humility for most Christians today isn't what they think. Modern-day humility does not resemble our advocacy or activism. It doesn't look like our monthly benevolent offering. It has no resemblance to our service in the church. It does not imitate the countless hours we give as a volunteer. None of these examples, although generous, equate to the humility that imitates Jesus Christ who had no worldly ambitions. Everything Jesus did was for the transformation and salvation of another soul. Jesus was on a soul-saving mission, by any means necessary, and although He was a star, He was not on a stardom tour.

"Before we whisper a prayer asking for humility, let us accept that the answer to our prayer may include some selfless sacrifices. This is what imitating Jesus Christ with humility looks like, but we have to be ready and willing."

We have to be careful about prayers that ask God to humble our spirit if we are not ready. These types of prayers can come with testing that will challenge us before God. So if we don't desire to mirror the humility of Jesus, then we should consider what we can live with in light of our ambitions and agendas. Jesus was human but also divine, and this means that He was capable of enduring trials and temptations unknown to us. We have to be mindful of our prayers, and they should always echo the thoughts of our hearts. But the prayer that we intend, must be the prayer that we pray. The prayer of our heart may be to put aside a spirit of haughtiness or boastfulness in areas where we have been notably successful. This means our humility becomes less about our elevation, and more about others' salvation. Therefore, before we whisper a prayer asking for humility, let us accept that the answer to our prayer may include some selfless sacrifices. This is what imitating Jesus Christ with humility looks like, but we have to be ready and willing. So when you pray, make sure it is an authentic reflection of your heart, and then prayerfully whisper, *God give me the right spirit.*

*Therefore, as God's chosen people, holy and dearly loved, clothe
yourselves with compassion, kindness, humility, gentleness,
and patience.*

Colossians 3:12

Prayer

*Father God, let me have the right spirit so that my service is
pleasing to you. God, may you receive all the glory for the works
of my hands and feet in this world. This is my prayerful whisper.
Amen.*

Reflection

Invite God into this moment. Think about your decision before
you ask God for the gift of humility.

What are you most ambivalent about when it comes to transforming your life in complete humility and service to God?

What sacred whisper would you like to share with God today?

GOD, CLEAR MY PLATE

In today's devotional moment with God, we talk about being spiritually stuck, and what we can do to be free of distractions. If you have ever heard yourself repeatedly whisper, *God, help me because this is too much,* then you are not alone. This is usually because we can't determine which projects should get the bulk of our attention, and which projects we should abandon. When we are over-committed it is difficult to determine what is the purpose-driven project. As a result, we waste valuable time spinning our wheels in vain.

Most of us want to walk in our purpose, but to do this, we need to know what our purpose looks like at every stage of our lives. What this means is that our purpose matures and develops just like we do. The older we become, the more evident our purpose becomes. When we can identify specific things that we do well, give us joy, or that we see as our passion, then it is a sign that our purpose has emerged and is ready to take form. This is why it is important to recognize that we truly were created with a purpose. God has instilled within each of us, unique skills, gifts, and talents that are foundational to our purposeful life.

"If we are to be effective in our purpose and calling, we too will need the Holy Spirit's guidance to solidify our purpose. This is how we begin to clear our plates and pursue our purpose."

A biblical example of understanding the meaning of being created with a purpose is captured in the story of the ascension of Jesus. As Jesus was preparing to ascend to heaven, He turned to His apostles and gave them their purpose to become the foundational builders of the Christian faith. Jesus wanted them to understand that the gift of God, which is the Holy Spirit, would be with them to guide them in fulfilling their purpose. He knew that for the apostles to be effective in their purpose and calling, they would need the Holy Spirit's guidance. If we are to be effective in our purpose and calling, we too will need the Holy Spirit's guidance to solidify our purpose. This is how we begin to clear our plates and pursue our purpose. We ask the Holy Spirit to guide our hearts and minds and order our steps.

All of the projects that are on our very full plates are nothing more than distractions that are hindering us from living a purposeful life. Our purposeful life allows us to do what God created us to do. In our sacred spaces, let us ask God to help us focus on our purpose and prayerfully whisper, *God, clear my plate.*

"All this I have spoken while still with you. But the Advocate, the Holy Spirit, whom the Father will send in my name, will teach you all things and will remind you of everything I have said to you.

John 14: 25-26

Prayer

Father God, help me to get rid of all distractions that keep me from focusing on my purpose and calling. God, I pray that I will have the discernment to recognize the signs of my emerging purpose and that the Holy Spirit will guide me to my purposeful life. This is my prayerful whisper. Amen.

Reflection

Invite God into this moment. Ask God what you need to do right now to get rid of all distractions.

How will you be intentional in pursuing the Holy Spirit's guidance, so that you can begin to give form to your purposeful life?

What sacred whisper would you like to share with God today?

GOD, KEEP ME FROM BECOMING SPIRITUALLY UNGLUED

In today's devotional moment with God, we talk through what it takes to prevent us from becoming spiritually unglued. Spiritual glue metaphorically is the faith that we have in God to hold us together emotionally and spiritually. It is the substance of our faith that has made our prayers work in a pinch and the power behind our petitions that stormed the throne of God.

In a moment of transparency, let's remember that there have been days when we struggled to get out of bed and leave the house. We didn't have the spiritual, emotional, or physical bandwidth to deal with people or do adulting. We didn't have the grace to handle the whiners at work, the stuff at school, or the cutoffs in our commutes. We didn't have the stamina for nonsense, the tolerance for foolishness, or the mercy for mess, but out of obligation we forced ourselves up and out the door anyway. Admittedly in hindsight, it was not that hard to become overwhelmed by life's expectations to be ever ready to be our best and do our best, so that people could see our best. Life was happening every moment, and it was hard to find time to be in our sacred space to reapply the spiritual glue that held us together. Before we knew it, we had become spiritually unglued and felt detached from God, even with faith as fervent as a mustard seed. This was not because there was a failure in our faith but because life had become unbalanced. We were choosing the grind over God.

> "The truth about God is that He will never leave us to fall apart without a plan to restore us."

God is the substance of our strength. He is the reason for our faith. God holds us together when everything and everyone else fails. The truth about God is that He will never leave us to fall apart without a plan to restore us. This is why God has to be the one that we adhere to. Today, as we meet this day with faith and assurance, let us prayerfully whisper, *God keep me from becoming spiritually unglued.*

*My flesh and my heart may fail, but God is the strength of my
heart and my portion forever.*

Psalm 73:26

Prayer

*Father God, you are the source of my strength and the strength
of my life. God, please be at my side so I will have the assurance
that all things will work out for my good at all times. This is my
prayerful whisper. Amen.*

Reflection

Invite God into this moment. What or who is holding you
together?

How can you allow God into your life as your source of
strength, and as the substance to firmly hold you together?

What sacred whisper would you like to share with God today?

GOD, HELP ME TO BE FOCUSED ON MY FAITH

In today's devotional moment with God, we talk through faith as a strategy for managing feelings of overwhelming dread. One of the tell-tale signs that a change in our perspective is badly needed is when we dread being in the same space or room with people that we prefer to keep at a distance. This feeling is comparable to those we had when we were children and were summoned to the principal's office, or when our boss asked if they could have a word with us. Yes, that feeling of dread! Dread, that has socialized and conditioned us to never want to feel this level of stress and anxiety again.

> "The withdrawal of emotions from any blind-sided event can help us focus. When we are focused, it helps us to reign in our emotions so that they mirror our best self or at least our brave self."

One of the reasons we experience dread is because there is no time to prepare for the content or context of the discussion or conversation in an impromptu meeting. We have no idea what will be said to us or happen in this encounter. Although we have life experience, there is no amount of professional training or people skills that can prepare us to meet this moment. So what do we do in situations like these? How do we handle the feelings of dread? We begin by focusing on what we can control, and this is our own heightened emotions. The withdrawal of emotions from any blind-sided event can help us to focus. When we are focused, it helps us to reign in our emotions so that they mirror our best self or at least our brave self. When we are focused, it helps us to see where we can be flexible, and where we need to stand our moral ground. In essence, focus is the key to unlocking our faith and faith keeps our fear in check.

With faith, we can manage our anxiety, stress, and the dread of facing our adversaries before we ever enter the room. These moments although terrifyingly dreadful are faith-molding moments. This is because God is giving us a seat at the table. Faith prepares us to walk in any room with our adversaries present and sit down in our spot and speak as a witness to the work of God within us. We handle dread by being focused on our faith. Today, prayerfully whisper, *God, help me to be focused on my faith.* Then trust God to answer the prayer.

Nevertheless, each person should live as a believer in whatever situation the Lord has assigned to them, just as God has called them.

1 Corinthians 7:17

Prayer

Father God, help me to be open to change and to be focused on my faith to see the blessing you have planned for me. This is my prayerful whisper. Amen.

Reflection

Invite God into this moment. What are you willing to do to change your response to situations and people you dread?

What do you need from God in making sustainable changes?

What sacred whisper would you like to share with God today?

GOD, FORGIVE ME
FOR NOT OBEYING

In today's devotional moment with God, we talk through life lessons on obedience. In personal reflection, whenever I and my siblings misbehaved as children, our parents would try very hard to correct our behavior with 'the look'. The 'look' was an intense stare that meant if we didn't self-correct our behavior immediately, there would be consequences later. Even at a young age, we understood that the authority of our parents was not to be challenged. They had rules for our family. These family rules were meant to keep us safe, provide a moral compass, and instill values of honesty and respect for God and others. We learned that these rules were foundational to the individuals we were to become, and our parents wanted to ensure that their children were ready to exist in a larger society. At the core of these rules were respect, honesty, ethical and moral behavior. We were socialized to function with these rules in mind, and not one of us wanted to disappoint or embarrass our family.

As we grew into adulthood, we realized that the rules given to us by our parents had successfully seeded a moral compass within us, and it always led us back to God. They had influenced and shaped their children into individuals who were capable of contributing well to society. Even when we fell short of our parents' expectations and stepped away from our moral compass, we learned to quickly seek forgiveness and prayer-fully whisper, *God, forgive me for not obeying*. Our prayers were life lessons on obedience, and these prayers would be asked again and again during our lifetime.

> "God is our heavenly Father and the parent who commands our obedience to this day. Therefore, in our sacred spaces, we can ask God to guide our lives with wisdom, grace, and love as our moral compass."

As adults the rules that guided us as children have been adapted to our social, emotional, and spiritual identity. We worry less about disappointing our parents but still have concerns about disappointing our family, friends, employers, and communities. Although we have learned to embrace our autonomy and have the freedom to make our own decisions about people and situations, the moral compass given to us as children remains compelling for the direction of our lives. This is because that moral compass always brings us back to God. God has always been a part of our upbringing. God is our heavenly Father and the parent who commands our obedience to this day. Therefore, in our sacred spaces, we can ask God to guide our lives with wisdom, grace, and love as our moral compass.

So be careful to do what the Lord your God has commanded you; do not turn aside to the right or the left. Walk in obedience to all that the Lord your God has commanded you, so that you may live and prosper and prolong your days in the land that you will possess.

Deuteronomy 5:32-33

Prayer

Father God, help me to not be so rigid with moral rules that govern my life that there is no room for your grace. God, I ask that you guide my life as a moral compass. This is my prayerful whisper. Amen.

Reflection

Invite God into this moment. What adjustments are you willing to make in your life to maintain your obedience to God?

How does your moral compass guide you as an adult who makes their own decisions?

What sacred whisper would you like to share with God today?

GOD, TAKE AWAY THE ADVERSARY'S OXYGEN

In today's devotional moment with God, we talk about dealing with the reality of spiritual warfare. As a personal example, Sunday mornings tend to be one of the most challenging days of the week for me. Every Sunday starts with me getting up three full hours before the weekly worship service. These three hours are especially filled with spiritual attacks. My preparation time for worship service is like *Murphy's Law* on steroids. Something unexpectedly falls or breaks. The worship music streaming on my artificial intelligence device suddenly stops working. The hot water tank for reasons unbeknownst to me is suddenly depleted, and this delays my shower and throws me off schedule. The combination of any of these incidents is enough to cause a level of frustration that makes me reconsider my decision to attend worship service at all. However, one Sunday morning it occurred to me that what was really happening was a full-blown spiritual attack. The irritation and frustration with these unexpected events were inadvertently giving the devil just what he needed, oxygen. It was a real revelation moment. The devil needs oxygen to breathe, and once he has it, he can turn a peaceful Sunday morning routine into total chaos. It was this revelation moment that caused me to prayerfully whisper, *God, take away the adversary's oxygen.*

> "When we are facing a spiritual attack, go into your sacred space, pray, and plan a counterattack. Then, draw near to God, resist the devil, withdraw his oxygen, and force him to flee."

The devil has an agenda for humanity, and it is to steal your peace, kill your hope, and destroy your life by disrupting your fellowship with God. When we understand that we are under spiritual attack, then we will be better prepared to defend ourselves. This defense includes petitions for God to command His angels to intercede and war on our behalf. God is in our sacred spaces, and it is where we go to prepare, plan, and pray for spiritual interventions that are strategic and precise. When we are facing a spiritual attack, we need to go into our sacred space, pray, and plan a counterattack. Then, draw near to God, resist the devil, withdraw his oxygen, and force him to flee.

Submit yourselves, then, to God. Resist the devil, and he will flee from you.

James 4:7

Prayer

Father God, help me to have the spiritual insight to know how to handle spiritual attacks. God, help me to draw near to you for shelter as you prepare me for a counterdefense. This is my prayerful whisper. Amen.

Reflection

Invite God into this moment. Ask God to help you recognize when you are being spiritually attacked, and to help you to resist the devil.

What can you do to be more prepared to fight spiritually against the schemes of the devil?

What sacred whispers do you want to share with God today?

PART II:
CONNECTION

CREATING CONNECTION THROUGH SACRED WHISPER

GOD, HELP ME OVERCOME ABANDONMENT

In today's devotional moment with God, we unpack our thoughts about abandonment and its residual impact on our lives. Abandonment is a tough topic because it is a painful experience to endure and overcome. When abandonment occurs in our lives it is usually without warning. We are generally unaware that something is wrong and are oblivious to the crisis brewing in the lives of the people we love. By the time we realize they are gone, our anxiety and grief have taken up residence and become our new companions. The challenge of abandonment is to avoid assigning blame to those who are still a part of our lives, and this includes God. In abandonment situations, it is easy to blame God for the list of actions we believe He should have taken to protect us. We have gone so far with blaming God that we have made Him as culpable as our deserter. Truthfully, God is omnipresent with an unrelenting love for every stage of our life.

> "We must trust that on the other side of every diffi-
> cult season in this life is God, and this is what we need
> to remember when life gives us painful experiences."

When we begin to process feelings of abandonment, what we are seeking to do is to make sense of it. We will often dissect our role in the relationship and question what we did or did not do, or what we said or failed to say. We assign blame to ourselves for missing possible warning signs. We do all of this in vain because we are on a mission to get a logical answer to why we have been abandoned. Yet, at the back of our minds is the belief that if we are not careful, our existing relationships may have the same fate. So what do we do with all of the unresolved thoughts and fears about abandonment? We do what is most comforting. We lean into the grace and guidance of a loving God and listen for clarity, comfort, and courage to reconcile what we cannot change. This is a reason to quietly retreat to our sacred spaces and prayerfully whisper, *God, help me overcome abandonment.* We must trust that on the other side of every difficult season in this life is God, and this is what we need to remember when life gives us painful experiences.

We are hard-pressed on every side, but not crushed;
perplexed, but not in despair.

2 Corinthians 4:8

Prayer

Father God, help me with issues of unresolved abandonment.
God, these issues are causing me to be fearful of forming trust-
worthy relationships. God, please help me to let the weight of
fear and anxiety go. This is my prayerful whisper. Amen.

Reflection

Invite God into this moment. What can you do to move into
a sacred space with God, so that you can process unresolved
abandonment, understand your value, and explore areas of
self-reconciliation?

What sacred whispers would you like to share with God today?

GOD, KEEP US ALL FROM HURT, HARM AND DANGER

In today's devotional moment with God, we unpack some of the lingering effects of abuse. The subject of abuse is difficult because it continues to be a taboo topic. Although it is happening daily in many parts of our world, it is not discussed often enough. This is because of the discomfort that people feel when hearing of domestic violence or emotional abuse incidents. We should not be surprised if there are some survivors of abuse reading or listening to this devotional. However, let it be boldly stated and affirmed that there is absolutely no reason, justification, or place for abuse in anyone's life. Inflicting physical, emotional, or verbal abuse upon another soul is sinful and intolerable. No one in God's creation deserves to experience abuse or live with the physical and emotional scars that remain, even when the assaults are over.

"Abuse is sin, and sin is the true source of any kind of suffering. However, God has reconciled our suffering through Jesus Christ. Jesus Christ has redeemed us all from the clutches of sin, and He did it with His life."

One of the most common practices of abuse occurs in plain sight. Verbal abuse is oftentimes subtle, and abusers have become experts at masking verbal attacks in settings that were once considered safe. Settings such as the workplace, school, or church. Although the depth of the verbal abuse may vary, the intent is to harm by calling into question a person's value or personal worth. Verbal abuse can also be masked by conversational tones. Although the voice inflection is calm, the words used are harsh and are meant to saturate the soul with the poison of prejudice. These harsh words are usually pointed and are intended to demean, belittle, or berate a person's character. The unfortunate truth is that it is beyond wrong. Abuse is shamefully sinful. Sinful because it is a transgression of the divine law of God. Divine law is what God has willed and revealed to all believers in scripture. Crucial to this revelation is that we love like God without conditions.

As believers, it is hard to make sense of why God would allow anyone to inflict or endure abuse. Although we may find it easier to blame God for the abuse we have suffered, we must reconcile that this was not God. This is not who God is to us. This is not what God desires for us. Abuse is sin, and sin is the true source of any kind of suffering. However, God has reconciled our suffering through Jesus Christ. Jesus Christ has redeemed us all from the clutches of sin, and He did it with His life. We have to intentionally make the choice for Jesus, and for salvation. God's promise is that in the coming age, sin will no longer exist, and neither will any suffering. But until that age, our faith has to be sufficient enough to provide us with the courage and the strength to retreat to safety at any time. In our sacred spaces as we pray for our family, friends, and neighbors' safety, let us prayerfully whisper, *God, keep us all from hurt, harm, and danger.*

But as for me, afflicted and in pain, may your salvation, God, protect me.

Psalm 69:29

Prayer

Father God, help me to resolve the grudges and unforgiveness I have in my heart for those who have hurt me. God, teach me to love as you love and forgive as you forgive so that I will experience your forgiveness and peace. This is my prayerful whisper. Amen.

Reflection

Invite God into this moment. How will you allow God to heal your wounds?

What do you need from God or others to move to a place of forgiveness?

What sacred whispers would you like to share with God today?

GOD, YOU'VE GOT THIS!

In today's devotional moment with God, we reflect on the conversation between God and Hezekiah. Hezekiah's story illustrates to us how we are to endure testing with faith. Hezekiah was the king of Judah and a devout servant of the Lord God. As the successor of his father King Ahab, who served pagan gods and killed the Lord's prophets, Hezekiah began his reign with a cleanse. Hezekiah destroyed all of the pagan shrines and altars, and the Asherah poles erected by his father and Queen Jezebel. He had taken swift action to affirm to the people and other kingdoms that he was faithful to the God of Abraham, Isaac, and Jacob. Consequently, Hezekiah endured a time of testing. Heavily reliant on his faith in God, the king had watched as the Assyrian army advanced and overtook Israel. He had paid a lofty ransom to the Assyrian King to save Judah. Despite this, Sennacherib, the King of Assyrian misread Hezekiah's faith and reliance on God as a lack of courage and strength. Nonetheless, Hezekiah remained confident and prayed to God for protection and preservation, and God did not allow them to be defeated or destroyed.

> "This is because when it comes to handling our enemies, only God can."

There are some things in life that we will not be able to handle on our own without the presence of God's supernatural power. This is because when it comes to handling our enemies, only God can. Hezekiah resisted taking matters into his own hands. He knew that there would be devastating consequences if he chose to move without God. Therefore, Hezekiah patiently waited in faith for God to respond to his prayers and petitions. Too often we become tired of waiting on God to answer our prayers, and we move into situations without God. What we learn from Hezekiah's story is that it is okay to be courageous, but without the supernatural power of God with us, our courage is misplaced. The lesson for us today is to know that God can rectify difficult situations in our lives. When we go into our sacred spaces with God and petition Him in faith for everything we need, we should believe in our prayerful whisper, *God, you have got this!*

And the Lord was with him; he was successful in whatever he undertook. He rebelled against the king of Assyria and did not serve him.

2 Kings 18:7

Prayer

Father God, give me the humility as a Christian to seek your guidance for situations in my life that are beyond my natural abilities. God, provide me with the gentle nudges needed to pray and petition you for what I need. This is my prayerful whisper. Amen.

Reflection

Invite God into this moment. Have you become overly confident in your identity as a Christian that you believe you have supernatural powers that are specific to God?

How will you handle teachings that tell you that God has equipped you to be His supernatural power source in the world?

What sacred whispers would you like to share with God today?

GOD, FIX THE SPIRITUAL SPLINTER

In today's devotional moment with God, we unpack the *spiritual splinters* that can create a disconnect from God. Has it ever occurred to us that there are some intense moments when we really need to hear from God? The intensity causes our prayers to become time-sensitive moments, and this means our petitions are for immediate answers. Prayers that are time-sensitive are usually related to crises, and human perception is that every crisis requires an immediate response. And not just any response, but a divine one. So what do we do when God is not responding quickly enough to our prayers? The answer is we pause, examine our relationship with God, and determine if our spiritual connection is strong. In other words, we perform our own spiritual diagnostic to determine whether spiritual splinters are creating a disruption.

Spiritual splinters are people, things, or situations that disrupt our connection with God by disrupting the amount of time we have reserved for Him. A spiritual diagnostic will identify lapses or changes in our bible study time, prayer life, and intimate quiet time alone with God. Whenever there is a spiritual disconnect, our first response should not be to panic but to repair it. Our focus should be on the repair and restoration of the relational issues that are creating the disruptions so that we can be reconnected quickly. Then, in our sacred spaces, we can prayerfully whisper, *God, fix the spiritual splinter.*

> "Spiritual splinters are people, things, or situations that disrupt our connection with God, by disrupting the amount of time we have reserved for Him."

We should all routinely perform a spiritual diagnostic. Just like we desire to be physically and emotionally healthy, we should also desire to be spiritually healthy. This means being attentive to the care and maintenance of our spiritual connection to God. Spiritual splinters do happen, but when we are connected to God, we have access to His plans, purpose, and priorities for our lives. Unanswered prayers do not mean that our prayers are ignored or denied but can be a sign that a spiritual diagnostic is needed. While we are in the diagnostic process, we must remember that God is always listening to our prayers, even when we have a spiritual splinter.

I call on you, my God, for you will answer me; turn your ear to me and hear my prayer.

Psalm 17:6

Prayer

Father God, help me to be connected to you in mind, body, and spirit. God, help me to see anything in my life that causes a spiritual splinter or disruptions in my relationship with you. This is my prayerful whisper. Amen.

Reflection

Invite God into this moment. Ask God if your unanswered prayers are indicators that some spiritual splinters are disrupting your connection.

What areas do you feel may need to be spiritually restored or reconnected?

What sacred whisper would you like to share with God today?

GOD, RELIEVE THIS SPIRITUAL BROKENNESS

In today's devotional moment with God, we unpack spiritual brokenness and the impact of the experience on our Christian identity. If we were to examine some of the underlying reasons for our spiritual brokenness, we would probably discover that a breach of our trust was a trigger event. When trust is breached, the residual effects can be devastatingly painful. This is because when it comes to personal experiences with those who identify as Christian, we have expectations. Expectations that we are safe and that any opposition or envy of our spiritual gifts is non-existent. Such expectations can lead us to idealize our relationships within the community of faith. This means we imagine situations and circumstances to be better than they are in reality. The problem with expectations and idealized perceptions is that they can cause us to miss red flags that signal something is wrong. And when we miss warning signs, it can cause us to become sheepishly vulnerable to spiritual attacks that wound and cause brokenness.

When we have been spiritually attacked and experience brokenness it is not the time to retreat and disconnect from God. In these moments of spiritual attack, our strategy should be to take refuge in our sacred spaces. Although we may be distraught, distressed, and disillusioned, we can still prayerfully whisper, *God, relieve this spiritual brokenness.*

"We can trust God with our spiritual brokenness and rely on Him to heal our hearts and mend our spirit."

The prayer for relief may take time but our response to our situation can be almost immediate. Some of us will not respond with brokenness but bitterness. Some of us will not respond as someone betrayed but bewildered. Some of us will not respond by asking for accountability but by accepting responsibility for ignoring our spiritual discernment. Whatever our response, we can trust God with our spiritual brokenness and rely on Him to heal our hearts and mend our spirits.

The Lord is close to the brokenhearted and saves those who are crushed in spirit.

Psalm 34:18

Prayer

Father God, help me seek you for healing during spiritual broken-ness. God, you are my healer and my peace. God, give me the courage to trust again and forgive. This is my prayerful whisper. Amen.

Reflection

Invite God into this moment. Ask God to help you process the residual effects of spiritual brokenness.

What do you feel are some of the issues that continue to affect how you engage people inside of the faith community?

What sacred whisper would you like to share with God today?

GOD, LET ME NOT BE MISUNDERSTOOD

In today's devotional moment with God, we unpack our experiences of being misunderstood. A common point of frustration for many Christians is having someone ask for an honest opinion when they really don't want one. Not every request for an opinion is a request for honesty. This is because honesty is not always appreciated, especially if it cannot be interpreted favorably. When our thoughts and opinions are solicited it is a delicate balance. This is because our thoughts and opinions need to be truthful, and not everyone can handle the truth when it is unfavorable.

As professed Christians, our faith should give us the courage to combat the fear of being transparent and truthful. Especially when it is not popular to be either. The truth is that as Christians, we have to adapt to the standards of our faith that were modeled by Jesus. We have to begin to be comfortable with being truthful. We have to understand that the truth will cause us to be misunderstood, mislabeled, and erroneously judged. We have to be our authentic selves as Christians, even if this means not fitting in. Jesus instructed us to be speakers of truth in every season and situation, and it is His opinion of us that should matter the most.

"When our thoughts and opinions are solicited it is a delicate balance. This is because our thoughts and opinions need to be truthful, and not everyone can handle the truth when it is unfavorable."

The problem is that truth and transparency are not subjective in the Christian context, and those seeking to be validated are not seeking to hear the truth. Although this may be difficult at the moment, we must remember to be honest and transparently truthful, even if it cannot be accepted. Therefore, let our prayerful whisper be, *God, let me not be misunderstood.*

The world cannot accept him because it neither sees him nor knows him. But you know him, for he lives with you and will be in you.

John 14:17

Prayer

Father God, help me to process the frustration and disappointment that comes with being misunderstood in moments of transparent honesty. This is my prayerful whisper. Amen.

Reflection

Invite God into this moment. Ask God to help you process the personal frustrations you may experience when you are disregarded for your transparent honesty.

Ask yourself what approach you will take in the future when you are asked to provide an opinion about a situation, experience, or person.

What sacred whisper would you like to share with God today?

GOD, HELP ME
UNDERSTAND WHY

In today's devotional moment with God, we unpack the purpose of asking God *why* questions. When it comes to the senseless things that happen in our world, why is the one question that is left unanswered. Yet, we continue to ask our political and religious leaders for a rational explanation to the societal ills of our world. We question why babies die at birth or children suffer from sickness and disease. We question why mass shootings happen in our schools, churches and grocery stores. We question why bad things happen to good people. We even question why perpetrators who have inflicted suffering appear to go unscathed. For every person who is angry or grieved or sick or suffering, why is the question they want answered.

The truth is why questions are reserved for an omniscient God. God has the answers to all of humanity's questions, and the answers may or may not be revealed in our lifetime. However, asking God is not an effort in vain, because He cares and comforts us even when life doesn't make sense.

> "The truth is why questions are reserved for an omniscient God. God has the answers to all of humanity's questions, and the answers may or may not be revealed in our lifetime."

The unfortunate truth is that we have no supernatural insight or ability to cure or resolve our fate. We have only human wisdom and knowledge. Our capacity to comprehend the divinity of God in our physical world is simply beyond our created station. This is the reason the why questions have no definitive answer. However, God is sovereign, and although He knows and has our answers, He provides comfort and compassion and a sacred space where we can prayerfully whisper, *God, help me understand why.*

"For my thoughts are not your thoughts, neither are your ways my ways," declares the Lord.

Isaiah 55:8

Prayer

Father God, help me to seek you for the answers to the why questions that affect my life. God, it is your answers that provide revelation, wisdom, knowledge, and understanding, and give me peace. This is my prayerful whisper. Amen.

Reflection

Invite God into this moment. Ask God for a better understanding of *why* so much is happening in our world.

Based on your intimate moments with God, how will you respond to the unanswerable questions going forward?

What sacred whisper would you like to share with God today?

GOD, I FEEL RESENTFUL

In today's devotional moment with God, we unpack some of the reasons that we continue to hold on to resentment. One of the reasons people hold on to resentment is because they have either unmet personal or professional goals or both. The reason their goals were not realized or delayed was because of their own decisions. These decisions were usually a choice to sacrifice personal goals or ambitions through several seasons of life. Although blame was assigned to all the recipients of their time and support, they were also culpable. Culpable because it was a decision of their own choosing, and we should always own our choices.

When we freely chose to make sacrifices for someone else, we probably did so without any consideration of our own future goals and ambitions, and this was the perfect environment for resentment to develop. Choices and decisions that are focused on other people's needs instead of our own seem admirable initially but are unrealistic. This is because at the core of resentment are feelings of disappointment and anger over lost opportunities. Resentment happens in part because we have convinced ourselves that we were helping and supporting at a time when it was needed most. We reasoned that our time, priorities, and plans could wait. We adjusted our schedules and delayed opportunities that were key to our career goals and ambitions. Then without warning, we hear ourselves complaining in our sacred spaces and with prayerful whispers, *God, I feel resentful.*

"Understand that the time we commit to working through feelings of resentment, should not be focused on what someone received from us, but what we were willing to freely give to them by our own choice."

The experience of resentment is real and can take time to really work through. Understand that the time we commit to working through feelings of resentment should not be focused on what someone received from us, but on what we were willing to freely give to them by our own choice. Our thought process should establish a healthy self-awareness of our own needs, and our needs are equally, if not more important, than those we desire to support. By maintaining a healthy awareness of our needs, goals, and ambitions, we will be more apt to make decisions that are not as susceptible to the development of resentment.

Humble yourselves, therefore, under God's mighty hand, that He may lift you up in due time. Cast all your anxiety on Him because He cares for you.

1 Peter 5:6-7

Prayer

Father God, help me with areas of my life where there is resentment. God, let resentment not take root within me. This is my prayerful whisper. Amen.

Reflection

Invite God into this moment. Ask God to help you understand your feelings of resentment.

What will you do in the future to support others while operating with boundaries that create a healthy balance?

What sacred whispers would you like to share with God today?

GOD, I AM INNOCENT

In today's devotional moment with God, we unpack the resolve it takes to overcome false accusations. When false accusations are launched into the public arena as truth, it is difficult for most people to be still and not mount a full-fledged defense. This is because our faith and discernment are edifying, and we understand that lies that are unchallenged can devastate and destroy lives. The perplexing thing about false accusations is that our accusers and adversaries know the truth but will perpetrate a lie as a part of a character assassination campaign.

The difficulty for anyone under a siege of false accusations is that we think we will have the support of our Christian colleagues. Unfortunately, this expectation is usually in vain. When we are under any kind of spiritual attack, the battle is against us and God, and others will not be aware of the spiritual warfare we are engaged in. We will be forced into a cycle of agonizing experiences that demand we defend our own character and integrity in every circle, including our Christian communities. Although it is a difficult experience, we will survive these vicious accusations because God will secure the victory on our behalf. Yet, the anguish that we will have to endure will take time. However, there is a place and space to shelter for moments of relief, and this is our sacred space where we can cry out in a prayerful whisper, *God, I am innocent.*

"Jesus confronted His accusers with the truth, not to convince or convict them of His innocence, but to expose their agenda to discredit Him."

As believers, we will be subjected to the scrutiny of our adversaries. It will not matter that we are known for our truthful transparency, because our adversaries will manipulate the truth to assassinate our character and witness. The question for us today is how are we to respond to false accusations. The answer is that we respond in the same way that Jesus did when He was falsely accused. Jesus confronted His accusers with the truth, not to convince or convict them of His innocence, but to expose their agenda to discredit Him. We will have to accept that our attempts to change our accusers' mind are a wasted effort because it does not align with their agenda to discredit us.

Jesus knew the power of the truth. He knew that truth has the power to free us from the anguish of being falsely accused. The truth will always prevail, and like Jesus, we will need to trust God in the process.

"Then you will know the truth, and the truth will set you free."

John 8:32

Prayer

Father God, help me to be patient and forgiving towards those who have falsely accused me of wrongdoing. God, thank you for the power and peace of the truth. This is my prayerful whisper. Amen.

Reflection

Invite God into this moment. How will you handle false accusers in your life?

What do you need from God to address the anguish caused by attacks on your integrity?

What sacred whispers would you like to share with God today?

GOD, LET THEM SEE YOU AND NOT ME

In today's devotional moment with God, we unpack how our servanthood has been challenged by pervasive suspicion within our communities. Have you ever attempted to help a stranger only to realize that the person you are trying to help is suspicious and questioning your motives? Unfortunately, their reaction to a random act of kindness has become far too familiar. This is because there is a great divide among people in our communities, and this includes believers and non-believers. People have become so untrusting that they are suspicious to the point of believing that their lives are in constant danger. This fear makes serving our communities extremely challenging, especially when we are trying to live as a servant of God.

Suspicion has complicated the servant's service and has given the devil a foothold to further divide. If the people of God are too frustrated or fearful to do the work of serving, then our efforts to expand the kingdom of God have been hindered. Further, when suspicion occurs without a logical reason, it is our darkest thoughts that prevent us from performing acts of service. We must be careful not to fall prey to the schemes of the devil. We must not incorrectly conclude that suspicion of us was based on something ugly like prejudice. Instead, we should prayerfully unpack our concerns in our sacred spaces and prayerfully whisper to *God, let them see you and not me.*

> "Everyone will not be content with our witness at work in the community, but it should not prevent us from serving."

Attempting to make sense of a person's suspicion is personally challenging. This is because it can cause us to project our own suspicion and incorrectly conclude that personal bias is the culprit. Unfortunately, when suspicion is not warranted, we are prone to make our conclusions, and this could increase the existing divide among us. Jesus and His disciples often had to face suspicion for their care of the sick, sinners, and the poor. The religious leaders constantly challenged Jesus and the disciples because of their care for these people groups, and as absurd as this was, it did not prevent them from serving. Everyone will not be content with our witness at work in the community, but it should not prevent us from serving. The encouragement for today's servant life is to remember that we have an assignment, and when we are met with suspicion, doing the will of God should continue to be our focus.

Offer hospitality to one another without grumbling. Each of you should use whatever gift you have received to serve others, as faithful stewards of God's grace in its various forms.

1 Peter 4:9-10

Prayer

Father God, help me to deal with the discomfort of others' suspicion of me and not take offense. This is my prayerful whisper. Amen.

Reflection

Invite God into this moment. Ask God to help you with the discipline needed to serve when facing suspicion.

How will you respond as a believer to those who are suspicious or fearful of your service to them?

What sacred whisper would you like to share with God today?

GOD, HELP ME WITH MY FRUSTRATION WITH PROCRASTINATION

In today's devotional moment with God, we unpack the behavior of procrastination and how it affects our lives and the lives of others. We may have had the experience of dealing with a procrastinator whose sense of urgency was nonexistent. When asked to help, we either gave or received the typical procrastinator response of "Yes, I'll help you later." We may have failed to recognize the response of procrastination until we were completely frustrated from waiting on the help promised.

Procrastination is not helpful to anyone trying to get something done. This is because assignments are never prioritized with tangible deadlines. The problem is that the promise to help never makes the procrastinator's to-do list or agenda, and this feels dishonest. Although this may not have been the procrastinator's intention, the outcome is a breach of the agreement to help. In these situations, our annoyance progresses from frustration to anger. The saving grace is that our sacred spaces are where issues with procrastination, breach of promise, and so much more get unpacked. We will just need to remember that unpacking issues is a process and not an event. Let us start the process of addressing procrastination in our sacred spaces with the prayerful whisper, *God, help me with my frustration and procrastination.*

> "As Christians, we have the guidance of scripture, and it reconciles that when we give our word, we give our commitment. This is what makes us different from people outside of the faith."

There are so many reasons people procrastinate. On the list of possible reasons is that they are overwhelmed in their own life and are unable to add another thing to their plate. Another possibility is not wanting to disappoint people by giving a no answer. Whatever the reason, procrastination is not a problem until a commitment is made and there is no actual action taken to satisfy the agreement. As Christians, we have the guidance of scripture, and it reconciles that when we give our word, we give our commitment. This is what makes us different from people outside of the faith. Therefore, if you struggle with procrastination, be aware that your decisions and unfulfilled commitments can be costly for you and others.

But I tell you that everyone will have to give account on the day of judgment for every empty word they have spoken. For by your words, you will be acquitted, and by your words, you will be condemned."

Matthew 12:36-37

Prayer

Father God, help me to overcome issues with procrastination so that I can be my best self, and not betray the trust of others in my life. This is my prayerful whisper. Amen.

Reflection

Invite God into this moment. Ask God to help you with areas of your life where you procrastinate.

How will you respond to those who need your help? How will assure them that they can trust you at your word to respond in the now?

What sacred whisper would you like to share with God today?

GOD, HELP ME TO NOT TAKE YOU FOR GRANTED

In today's devotional moment with God, we unpack the importance of not taking God for granted. The most significant relationship that we will ever have in this earthly life is the relationship for which we were created, and this is our relationship with God. Although it may be hard to imagine, our sovereign God created us to be in a relationship with Him. What makes God's choice surprising is the capacity of the human soul to be sinful. God knew that we would have the proclivity to be unreliable, disobedient, and obstinate toward His will. Yet, God entrusted us with the care of His creation and gave us dominion. Literally, we are God's choice as His relational companions, but instead of faithfully honoring this privilege, we have taken it for granted again and again.

> "The most significant relationship that we will ever have in this earthly life is the relationship for which we were created, and this is our relationship with God."

We may be surprised to learn that how we handle our people relationships is not all that different from how we manage our relationship with God. Although we may have some commitment to our relationships, they are far from *the laying down of our life's illustration* given by Jesus. We may be a person who is so entrenched with our own needs that we fail to be committed to the needs of our relationships. We may be so conditioned to receive support when we are distressed that we fail to recognize or reciprocate support. We may have learned how to have a friend but not how to be a friend. The unfortunate truth is that while all of these examples may not apply, some do. This is why we should evaluate the state of our relationship with God first and then with others.

When we are guilty of relational neglect, we cheat others in the relationship by withholding our time, attention, and concern. God is forgiving, but others, are not so much. This is because people rarely forget how we make them feel. For this reason, we should be committed to reconciling what is not mutually working. Then, in our sacred spaces prayerfully whisper, *God, help me to not take you for granted.* Today may be an opportune time for us to reset how we approach all of our relationships, especially our relationship with God.

Do nothing out of selfish ambition or vain conceit. Rather, in humility value others above yourselves, not looking to your interests but each of you to the interests of the others.

Philippians 2:3-4

Prayer

Father God, help me to be less focused on my own needs so that I can extend my love and support to others who are mutually engaged in a relationship with me. Show me how to be relational as you intended. This is my prayerful whisper. Amen.

Reflection

Invite God into this moment. What will you do to reset your relational instincts?

What will help you approach your relationship with God and others more mutually?

What sacred whisper would you like to share with God today?

GOD, HELP ME OVERCOME BETRAYAL

In today's devotional moment with God, we begin the process of unpacking betrayal. If we were to survey a group of friends, we would probably discover that most of them have had the misfortune of being a victim of betrayal. Betrayal is one of the most painful experiences we can have with another person. This is because we never saw it coming. We were unaware that the conditions of our relationship had changed, and that the new agenda to betray us had been instituted. As such, we continued to believe and behave as if the original agenda was still operating. We held firm to the belief that their intentions were to be supportive, an advocate, and a friend. We believed that they would continue to be trustworthy and dependable and keep our confidence. The reason we believed this is because there were no red flags or whispers or changes in behavior that signaled something was different, and they made their lies sound convincingly like the truth. It was only when things unraveled that we were able to scramble to the safety of our sacred spaces to deal with the pain of betrayal. In the comforting presence of God, we were able to gather ourselves and prayerfully whisper, *God, help me overcome betrayal.*

> "We overcome betrayal by exposing the hidden agendas of our betrayers, and by withdrawing their access to a relationship with us. Then, we allow God to heal our hearts, walk us through the process of forgiveness, and restore our trust."

Betrayal has a way of coloring the lens of our existing and new relationships. This is because the pain of betrayal can linger, and this can cause us to be overly cautious. Even our efforts to transition into emotional spaces where we can trust again are challenging. The encouraging news is that overcoming betrayal is possible, and we only need to look to Jesus for a tangible example.

Jesus knew Judas Iscariot would betray Him, but the invitation to be one of the twelve was extended to him anyway. Jesus' strategy in dealing with betrayal was to confront the hidden agenda of his betrayer. By exposing Judas Iscariot, he was no longer able to pretend to be someone he was not, nor was he welcomed to continue in the relationship. What Jesus taught us is that we overcome betrayal by exposing the hidden agendas of our betrayers, and by withdrawing their access to a relationship with us. Then, we allow God to heal our hearts, walk us through the process of forgiveness, and restore our trust.

*Let us not become weary in doing good, for at the proper time
we will reap a harvest if we do not give up.*

Galatians 6:9

Prayer

*Father God, I am still hurting from betrayal. God, I need your
compassion, grace, and mercy to move past this painful time and
ask that you bless me now. This is my prayerful whisper. Amen.*

Reflection

Invite God into this moment. Ask God to strengthen you emotionally and spiritually.

Can you give yourself permission to let go of the woundedness
of betrayal and move forward?

What else will you need from God?

What sacred whisper would you like to share with God today?

GOD, HELP ME COPE WITH SPIRITUAL SADNESS

In today's devotional moment with God, we unpack some of the reasons we have periods of spiritual sadness. In a personal reflection, I acknowledge that I am not a licensed mental health professional. However, my professional experiences with supporting others dealing with periods of *spiritual sadness* are specific to my education and clinical training as a Professional Chaplain and Pastoral Counselor. It is from these experiences that spiritual sadness is differentiated from other forms of clinical sadness.

When we experience sadness as a normal and emotional response, it is usually caused by an incident with an unwanted outcome. We may be sad because we didn't get the promotion. We may be sad because of a personal disagreement. We may be sad because of a missed opportunity. In other words, there is a reason for our feelings of sadness, and when we are aware of its causes, then it is easier to identify a solution. The same resolve can be applied to the experience of spiritual sadness.

> "At the heart of practicing Christians is the desire
> for a connected relationship with God. God is the
> source of all of our needs and when we can connect in
> meaningful ways, then we can process all of our
> experiences, including periods of spiritual sadness."

Spiritual sadness is an emotional response triggered by feelings of being spiritually separated from God. This means that as members of the family of God, we emotionally experience an absence of God's omnipresence. This experience also creates feelings of being detached and disconnected from God, and this is the primary reason for our sadness. We may not have been able to name it at the time, but these descriptors are synonymous with the experience. When we are dealing with spiritual sadness, we have no specific cause that we can point out that triggered the spiritual sadness that we feel. This is what makes spiritual sadness difficult to process. Unlike its cousin, emotional sadness, spiritual sadness happens without warning, and its onset is the sudden and immediate experience of feeling detached and disconnected from God's presence.

So what do we do about spiritual sadness? We address spiritual sadness by rebooting our spiritual disciplines and practices. Our spiritual disciplines like prayer, praise, and worship allow us to connect and communicate with God. However, like other disciplines and practices used to maintain a healthy mind, body, and spirit, we must routinely assess their effectiveness. Otherwise, they can become rote and ineffectual.

At the heart of practicing Christians is the desire for a connected relationship with God. God is the source of all of our needs and when we can connect in meaningful ways, then we can process all of our experiences, including periods of spiritual sadness. Our sacred spaces are where we should begin the process of rebooting, and start with the prayerful whisper, *God help me cope with spiritual sadness.*

The precepts of the Lord are right, giving joy to the heart. The commands of the Lord are radiant, giving light to the eyes.

Psalm 19:8

Prayer

Father God, help me to resolve these feelings of spiritual sadness and separation from you. God, guide me as I pursue you with my whole heart and draw near to you once more. This is my prayerful whisper. Amen.

Reflection

Invite God into this moment. Ask yourself if your spiritual disciplines and practices are active and effective.

Do you believe your spiritual disciplines are enough to address spiritual sadness and other issues affecting your hope and joy?

What sacred whisper would you like to share with God today?

GOD, PLEASE BE MY LISTENING EAR AND SOUNDING BOARD

In today's devotional moment with God, we unpack the importance of having God as our listening ear and sounding board. Everyone has a story. We have all experienced good times and bad times. We have all had pinnacle moments and valley-low periods. We have celebrated achievements, births, graduations, marriages, and milestones. We have captured memories and savored victories. All of these experiences have become a part of our story. Like most stories, our experiences have become a collage of our lives. We look forward to personal and intimate opportunities to share our stories with our support circles. However, the challenge that many will face today is that our support circles may not be willing to be a listening ear or sounding board. This is because they fear being made aware of personal adversities that may be too heavy for them emotionally. The responsibility of carrying the weight of unresolved trauma or pain is lofty, so our support circles may become avoidant to difficult conversations. For us, this may be frustrating and seem selfish at first glance, but for others, it is a model of good self-care.

"When we provide a listening ear and sounding board, we are not being asked to provide a solution. We are being asked for a safe space to attentively listen to a person's experiences or thoughts."

If you have ever wondered why people find it so difficult to be a listening ear or sounding board, it is probably because many people have been socially conditioned to believe that the sharing of adverse experiences burdens the listener. This social conditioning has failed to differentiate between listening to a person process their thoughts out loud and being a listening ear for someone's unfortunate experiences. When we provide a listening ear and sounding board, we are not being asked to provide a solution. We are being asked for a safe space to attentively listen to a person's experiences or thoughts. Unfortunately, some of those within our trusted support circles misunderstand what we are asking of them. This is why we must clearly state what is needed to prevent avoidance from developing in the relationship. The goal is never to lose our support system but to complement the spiritual support we already have with God.

The good news is that God is near to us and is always available to be our listening ear and sounding board. This is why we have the privilege of our sacred spaces, because within this space we can be heard and understood. Then, as needed, prayerfully whisper, *God, please be my listening ear and sounding board.*

This is the confidence we have in approaching God: that if we ask anything according to His will, He hears us. And if we know that He hears us—whatever we ask—we know that we have what we asked of Him.

1 John 5:14-15

Prayer

Father God, I pray that you will make me aware of any social conditioning that would cause me to be unavailable to those who need to be heard. God, help me to show care and concern for those needing to be comforted and encouraged in their life. This is my prayerful whisper. Amen.

Reflection

Invite God into this moment. Can you be open to listening actively to someone who needs this type of support?

What social conditioning has affected your ability to be available to someone in need?

What sacred whisper would you like to share with God today?

GOD, GUARD ME AGAINST DISTRACTIONS

In today's devotional moment with God, we unpack distractions and how they can create delays in achieving our divine purpose. Our Western culture prides itself on efficiency. We are people who take pride in our ability to successfully multi-task seamlessly. For some, the younger and more energetic version of ourselves was above proficient at multitasking. We had a rhythm, and we didn't want anything to interrupt our multi-tasking flow. We could manage the multiple demands of our careers, families, friends, and finances, as long as there were no unanticipated distractions to disrupt our focus. It was only age, time, and experience that caused a shift in our multi-tasking mindset. At some point, we became aware that we were so enamored with our dynamic multi-tasking skills, that we had not given ourselves time to focus on achieving our divine purpose.

"This is why we have to be mindful of distractions, because when left unchecked, they can keep us from giving God our full attention, and without His counsel and guidance our divine purpose cannot be achieved."

Many of us have no revelation of our divine purpose. We have been so distracted with being efficient in our lives and careers that we have left no space to connect with God. Connecting with God is how we gain clarity, and an awareness of our divine purpose. It is how we become aware of what we were created to do, and who we were created to be. This is why we have to be mindful of distractions, because when left unchecked, they can keep us from giving God our full attention, and without His counsel and guidance our divine purpose cannot be achieved. Connecting daily with God in our sacred spaces is a new opportunity to process distractions and all other hindrances. Therefore, let our prayerful whisper be, *God, guard me from distractions.*

She had a sister called Mary, who sat at the Lord's feet listening to what He said. But Martha was distracted by all the preparations that had to be made.

Luke 10:39

Prayer

Father God, I pray that I will not become so distracted with multi-tasking that I ignore you and my divine purpose. I pray that you will help me to not miss the moments that matter. This is my prayerful whisper. Amen.

Reflection

Invite God into this moment. Ask God to help you with distractions related to being a multi-tasker.

What distractions are keeping you from achieving your divine purpose?

What does God want you to re-evaluate in your life?

What sacred whisper would you like to share with God today?

GOD, THANK YOU FOR NOT REJECTING ME

In today's devotional moment with God, we unpack some of the reasoning behind rejection. Rejection for most people is unavoidable. This is because we cannot make anyone accept who we are as a person. There may be characteristics about our personality that just don't click with other people. Some may not appreciate our transparency, honesty, assertiveness, or whatever makes us different or our unique selves. Although rejection is never a pleasant experience, we are able to navigate around these feelings because we don't want them to be paralyzing for us. On the other hand, when rejection happens in certain settings it can become an emotional boulder that we have a hard time moving past. This is especially true when rejection happens in the church or any other setting that we have deemed sacred or safe.

> "We each have our own gifts, skills, talents, and charisma, and if we were more willing to look at others through this lens, then we would discover that those we find different lean toward Jesus Christ as much as we do."

At the heart of rejection is the issue of comparison. The truth is that we reject people because of their differences. As Christians, we have been taught to adopt, practice, and follow the teachings of Jesus Christ. This means that we don't reject people. This is because rejection equates to exclusion, and denying people access because of differences is never okay. Our role is to provide opportunities for inclusion so that anyone who desires can be a part of the family of God through Jesus Christ. The truth about Christians is that we are imperfect people who are striving to adhere to the divine law of a perfect God. We want people to adopt a lifestyle that we believe is authentically Christian, and we want to decide. However, until we as Christians are able to reconcile that there is nothing wrong with being different, then we will continue to struggle with rejection.

Rejection will then continue to tap into our fear of not being enough. Each of us is uniquely and intentionally created by God to be different. There is not an identical replica of us anywhere. Our differences are not a mistake or an error. We each have our own gifts, skills, talents, and charisma, and if we were more willing to look at others through this lens, then we would discover that those we find different lean toward Jesus Christ as much as we do. Christians share faith, and it is what makes us one body. Therefore, let us be mindful of comparisons that cause us to reject others, and with the grace given to us prayer-fully whisper, *God, thank you for not rejecting me.*

Though my father and mother forsake me, the Lord will receive me.

Psalm 27:10

Prayer

Father God, I pray that my heart will be open to those who are different. Let me not reject others because of my own need to be accepted. This is my prayerful whisper. Amen.

Reflection

Invite God into this moment. How will you stand against exclusionary practices in your workplace, peer group, family, or faith community?

What steps will you take to combat biases that lead to rejection?

What sacred whisper would you like to share with God today?

GOD, HELP ME MOVE TO A PLACE OF RESPONSIBILITY

In today's devotional moment with God, we unpack some of the thought processes behind the reasons people refuse to accept responsibility for their actions. Accepting responsibility for one's actions is not something that readily happens in our culture anymore. There was a time when any social offense towards another person was followed by an immediate apology. No one wanted to be labeled as arrogant, rude, or disrespectful. People were uncomfortable and embarrassed by their inappropriate interactions, attitudes, and behaviors. So much so that inappropriate interactions and responses were noted as 'socially incorrect' or 'politically incorrect'. This cultural vernacular meant that a person was behaving in a way that was unacceptable according to our social norms.

As subtle as it was, a cultural shift happened, and our attitudes changed. We became people with personalities that were driven towards self-sufficiency and success, or in the language of this cultural context 'winning'. We were emboldened to speak our truth with no trepidation or regard for whether it was received as rude or disrespectful. We were good with forgoing politeness and courtesies in exchange for the perception of being a 'boss'. We ascribed to a posture of denying responsibility for our words or actions because we were labeled 'fierce'. We were comfortable with the misrepresentation of 'no harm, no foul' because we saw no need. With this mentality in full regalia, we failed to pause, pivot, and plead with God in our sacred spaces. When we become subjected to the confines of our culture, this is when we need to take a breath and prayerfully whisper *God, help me move to a place of responsibility.*

> "When we cause harm by our words or actions, we should assume sole responsibility, and look for opportunities to be reconciled."

If we prescribe to the mentality that personal responsibility should be shared, even in cases when we have disregarded the basic social norms, then we have grossly misread the situation. One of the relational practices of Jesus Christ was to respect everyone's position in life. He was often witnessed to socialize with those on the fringes of society such as women, tax collectors, and lepers. Jesus Christ did this so that His followers would understand that everyone has value and should be respected and regarded as such. When we cause harm by our words or actions, we should assume sole responsibility, and look for opportunities to be reconciled. Ultimately, we are all responsible for transforming our social norms to be a culture of mutual respect and responsibility.

Let your conversation be always full of grace, seasoned with salt, so that you may know how to answer everyone.

Colossians 4:6

Prayer

Father God, I pray to be more intentional with my respect for others. God, help me to be quick to seek forgiveness and reconciliation for any offense I may have caused. This is my prayerful whisper. Amen.

Reflection

Invite God into this moment. Ask yourself if you are someone who readily takes responsibility for words and actions that have offended others.

How will you be more attentive to respecting others regardless of their position in life?

What sacred whisper would you like to share with God today?

GOD, THEY ARE NOT QUALIFIED TO JUDGE ME

In today's devotional moment with God, we unpack the reasons we have no qualifications to judge another soul. We all know the looks. The disapproving stares, quick glances, or the brief grumbles that non-verbally note disapproval. These non-verbal cues signal that we are the current target of someone's judgment. Within minutes of entering a space, we have the feeling that we don't belong nor are we welcome. For reasons unbeknownst to us, we are immediately judged and almost instinctively we begin to second-guess our choices. We critique the garments we are wearing or the fragrance that scents our space. We question whether our brief words were too much or if our body language is the wrong vibe. We begin to process the color of our clothing, the length of our hair, the style of our shoes, down to the very detail until we have exhausted every possible reason to be the subject of someone's judgment. Unfortunately, this self-critiquing behavior is as unconscious as the non-verbal apology we will give for not meeting the standards of our judges. Although this makes no rational sense, it is a ritual that we will repeat again.

The breakthrough from this unconscious reaction to judgment has to be intentional. We have to decide that people who have inserted themselves into our lives as our judges are not qualified to hold the position. When we remove their perceived authority, then we will have the confidence to process in our sacred spaces our reactions and affirm with a prayerful whisper, *God, they are not qualified to judge me.*

"We need to rejoice in the grace of God because there is no one on this earth who possesses the credentials to judge us."

The biblical story of Jesus' defense of a woman caught in an act of adultery is to teach us that anyone who assumes the position of judge must be qualified. Jesus defines this qualification as possessing a high moral character that is unblemished. In other words, only those who are sinless meet the criteria to judge sinners. Jesus who is not defending the woman's sin, but her right to be judged by those qualified, establishes the measurement for judgment. To His point, no sinner can judge another because neither is qualified. In light of this revelation, we need to rejoice in the grace of God because there is no one on this earth who possesses the credentials to judge us.

"Do not judge, or you too will be judged. For in the same way you judge others, you will be judged, and with the measure you use, it will be measured to you.

Matthew 7:1-2

Prayer

Father God, I acknowledge that I am a sinner and this makes me unqualified to judge anyone. God, I ask for your forgiveness for every time I have judged others, and for the strength to not repeat this sinful behavior. This is my prayerful whisper. Amen.

Reflection

Invite God into this moment. Ask God to help you to not judge others.

How will you manage your reactions to people knowing that you are not qualified to judge them?

What sacred whisper will you share with God today?

GOD, JEALOUSY IS NOT LIKE YOU

In today's devotional moment with God, we unpack perceptions that can cause jealousy. Jealousy is a hard conversation but one that we need to have. As hard as it may be to admit, we have probably all experienced being jealous of someone. Before you close today's devotional in disagreement, reflect back on a time when you or someone you knew was jealous of a person in their social circle. This person was envied because of their accomplishments. They lived in an affluent neighborhood, owned luxury cars, held an executive position in their career field, and were equivalent to their spouse or partner in every way. Yet, regardless of their successes, they remained friends with their peer group. Their behavior didn't change but other members of the group behaved differently towards them. This was because they were jealous. Although some would probably deny it, it was their behavior that caused the person to disconnect and disassociate from the group.

Jealousy is a normal human behavior, but it can cause people to be cruel and hurtful. Although jealousy is largely based on perception, it stirs the soul's insecurities to project unwarranted feelings and thoughts. This is why we must be careful with how we manage our perceptions because perceptions have the propensity to choose targets of envy.

> "Jealousy happens because we have accepted our perceptions as our reality. We have convinced our-selves that we are not as accomplished, valuable, respected, or appreciated as our colleagues and peers."

Some of the reasons we experience jealousy are because of our personal insecurities, but also because of the vanity around losing our significance in our sphere of influence. Jealousy happens because we have accepted our perceptions as our reality. We have convinced ourselves that we are not as accomplished, valuable, respected, or as appreciated as our colleagues and peers. When our perceptions have taken control, this is when we need to shift our focus and energy upward to connect with God. God is our source of life and gives us the guidance and support needed to reign in our perceptions. This is so that we can thwart envy from developing within our spirits. When the desires of our heart are placed by God, it allows us to see our own value, and how valuable we are to Him. Therefore, in our sacred spaces we can repent for our envy and prayerfully whisper, *God, jealousy is not like you.*

Since we live by the Spirit, let us keep in step with the Spirit. Let us not become conceited, provoking, and envying each other.

Galatians 5: 25-26

Prayer

Father God, I admit that there have been times when I have been jealous and envious of other people because of my insecurities. God, renew the right spirit in me so that I am grateful for who you created me to be. Help me to appreciate my connection with you each day. This is my prayerful whisper. Amen.

Reflection

Invite God into this moment. Ask God for the discerning wisdom to appropriately address negative perceptions.

What strategy will you use to manage feelings of jealousy and envy towards others?

How will you validate your own value? What will you need?

What sacred whispers would you like to share with God today?

GOD, PLEASE TAKE AWAY THE FEAR OF BEING MISLED

In today's devotional moment with God, we unpack the experience of being misled. Familiarity with people happens over time and develops as we socialize in personal, professional, and faith group settings. Personal interactions that occur regularly help us to become comfortable and familiar with people who are new to us. When we can associate people's names with their faces, and their personalities with both, then familiarity has occurred. But this does not mean that we will be able to provide a character reference or validate their trustworthiness. This is because they are only superficially familiar to us, and we have no experience with how they may handle our personal confidentiality.

Trust is a huge keystone of a relationship. It should only be given to those who have the integrity to manage it. When we give our trust to a person, this means that they have been elevated from a familiar acquaintance to a trusted friend who is capable of handling our privacy. They are invited and accepted within our trust circle, and we freely interact with them without extreme caution. This is because our fear of harm has been minimalized by our interpersonal experiences. But, the unfortunate thing about trusted friends is that they are flawed individuals like us, and as a result may intentionally or unintentionally breach our trust which can cause us to feel misled.

> "Trust is a huge keystone of a relationship. It should only be given to those who have the integrity to manage it. When we give our trust to a person, this means that they have been elevated from a familiar acquaintance to a trusted friend who is capable of handling our privacy."

There is an extraordinary group of people who operate contrary to this social norm of *'show me I can trust you.'* What makes this group of people special is that they seem to have no sense of alarm about trusting new people. They are not cautiously guarded, have no fear of being deceived or misled, and are thought to have never met a person they would call a stranger. Although this might seem naive, they have the unique gift of relational connection that we see in the life of Jesus. They seem to understand how Jesus was able to connect with the multitudes in one moment and the pharisee in the next. Seemingly, Jesus' model of being accepting of all kinds of people works for them, because it worked for Him. The point is that our past pain can create cautionary instincts. We must begin to resolve hurt and reign in our fear of being misled. Our fear can be paralyzing and can keep us from imitating Jesus' life. We can begin to address our fear in our sacred spaces with prayerful whispers, *God, please take away the fear of being misled.*

In you, Lord my God, I put my trust. I trust in you; do not let me be put to shame, nor let my enemies triumph over me.

Psalm 25:1-2

Prayer

Father God, trusting you means everything to me. God, I know with your help I can overcome my fear of being misled and learn how to trust with your guidance. This is my prayerful whisper. Amen.

Reflection

Invite God into this moment. What will help you to be more open to engaging in new relationships?

What will help you to ease your guardedness towards people who are unfamiliar to you?

What sacred whisper would you like to share with God today?

GOD, LET ME DEMONSTRATE PATIENCE WHEN I AM HANDLED

In today's devotional moment with God, we unpack our human response to being handled by others. It doesn't take us very long to figure out when someone is attempting to handle us or is handling someone else. This is because they immediately assume our voice. They do this by interrupting and interjecting themselves into our conversations, thought processes, and opinions as a way to control the situation. The purpose of having control is so that they can change the narrative and influence the audience into adopting their agenda.

What is often misinterpreted by onlookers is that the person being handled agrees with this behavior, when in actuality they are a victim of circumstance. The person being handled may have been blindsided by an invitation that appeared innocent and credible. They may have trusted someone involved in organizing the event. They may have thought the cause was worthy of their support. Whatever the reason for their initial voluntary participation, they were unaware that they would be handled. Oftentimes the person being handled is struggling to recover control of their voice, and their silence gives the appearance of agreement when this is not the case. The truth is that when someone is being handled, it means that they are being exploited.

"When our rights are exploited because someone has kidnapped our voice, and is handling us, our response to these environments should remain consistent with our Christian witness."

As human beings, each of us was given by God our free will. This means that we have the right to make our own choices, choose our own words, and make our own definitive decisions. When our rights are exploited because someone has kidnapped our voice and is handling us, our response to these environments should remain consistent with our Christian witness. Although we won't appreciate the handler's disingenuous and controlling behavior in those moments, we must align our words with the wisdom of God. This means that we will have to decide whether to respond instinctively, patiently, or with great restraint. In moments of exploitation, it can be difficult to think clearly, and although we may desire to protect our Christian witness, our restraint will be tested. Our sacred spaces are safe places of preparation and are where we process the prayerful whisper, *God let me demonstrate patience when I am handled.*

See to it that no one takes you captive through hollow and deceptive philosophy, which depends on human tradition and the elemental spiritual forces of this world rather than on Christ.

Colossians 2:8

Prayer

Father God, help me with my desire to temper my responses with wisdom and not anger. God, let nothing tear me apart from you. This is my prayerful whisper. Amen.

Reflection

Invite God into this moment. Ask God to teach you how to operate graciously and patiently toward others when they are attempting to handle you.

How can you use patience, so it becomes your greatest strength?

What sacred whisper would you like to share with God today?

GOD, GRANT ME YOUR PROTECTION

In today's devotional moment with God, we unpack our fears, and how we can confront it with courageous faith. As hard as this is to admit, everyone has a fear of something. It could be a fear of a reptile, rodent, stranger, or the unknown. As such, many of us will take precautionary measures to avoid dangerous situations where we don't feel safe and protected. This includes adjusting our lifestyles by changing our routines, equipping ourselves with protective gear, or taking a self-defense course. We will do all of this in preparation to protect ourselves from physical harm and danger. Although this sounds over the top for some people, it is a necessity for others. However, with all this protective preparation there is still a real danger that most of us rarely consider, and that is the danger of a spiritual assault in a natural world.

> "God is our strong tower and our safety and protection. This is why we can find solace in our sacred spaces, because our God, affirms that He is working things out for our good and is defending and defeating."

The danger of a spiritual assault is real. What makes it real is the increasing presence of sinfulness and Godlessness in our world. People are no longer timid with their atheist or agnostic viewpoints. They openly and often deny the existence of the Almighty God. As such, each day the media reports tragedies perpetrated at the hands of mankind. Oftentimes when we focus on tragic events, we hear that they seemed unprovoked, random, and without reasonable explanation. Although you as readers or listeners of this devotional may disagree, these events are consistent with the prevalence of sin in the form of a spiritual attack in our world.

When we are attacked spiritually, it initially can seem subtle. We may notice a pivotal change in our interactions and in our environment. We may experience frequent opposition to everything we do, and everything we believe. There may even be questions challenging our faith. How we recognize spiritual attacks is to question whether there has been a pivotal change towards us, adversarial responses to us, and a challenge to test our faith to cause us to forfeit or lose. If any of these issues are present, it is important to turn our focus to God. This is why we can find solace in our sacred spaces, because our God, affirms that He is working things out for our good and is defending and defeating. When we experience physical or spiritual danger, we have to move forward with courageous faith and prayerfully whisper, *God, grant me your protection.*

The name of the Lord is a fortified tower; the righteous run to it and are safe.

Proverbs 18:10

Prayer

Father God, thank you for the peace and the protection that you give to me, and to all those I love. God, I am grateful that you keep watch over me day and night, and protect me from all hurt, harm, and danger. God sound the alarm so that I know when to shelter under your mighty wing. This is my prayerful whisper. Amen.

Reflection

Invite God into this moment. What will you do to activate your faith and have the peace of mind that God is protecting you?

How will you respond to others who don't believe in the power of your faith?

What sacred whisper would you like to share with God today?

GOD, BE MY FIRST PRIORITY

In today's devotional moment with God, we unpack the need to prioritize God in our lives. Unquestionably, God should be our first priority. Every rising in the morning, and resting in the evening should be carefully considered with God. This is because when hardships happen and crisis comes, God will be the first to hear from us. Yet, when our life is at its best, this is when we struggle to prioritize God above everything else. Every earthly relationship we will have with another human soul will change because people change. However, God will never change. What is at the root of our struggle to prioritize our relationship with God? The answer may be that we have not thoroughly evaluated nor prioritized our needs.

When we have full plates, it is important to recognize that everything that we have piled onto our proverbial plate will require a decision. This means that everything on the plate will need to be evaluated, prioritized, and decided. The criterion for this evaluation is to process how it will impact our physical, mental, and spiritual well-being, and if the impact will have a positive or negative effect. This is because the decision-making process identifies priorities based on our needs and categorizes them in the order of most importance to our lives at any time.

"When we prioritize our lives, we have to be deliberate with our decisions because they will either compete or connect."

When we prioritize our lives, we have to be deliberate with our decisions because they will either compete or connect. When our decisions connect, we are able to categorize our needs in order of priority. But when our decisions compete, there is no priority, because we have decided that everything is important. The reality is that we will have to deliberately decide that God is our priority. This is because He provides for all of our needs regardless of how they are ranked and categorized.

We handle our very full lives of duties and responsibilities with decisions that have been thoroughly considered in our sacred spaces with God. Then, when there are decisions to be made, we can prayerfully whisper, *God, be my first priority.*

Without delay, he called them, and they left their father Zebedee in the boat with the hired men and followed him.

Mark 1:20

Prayer

Father God, let me never hesitate to follow you as my priority. God give me the wisdom and guidance to make decisions aligned with your will for me. This is my prayerful whisper. Amen.

Reflection

Invite God into this moment. Evaluate your priorities that compete with God. What changes are you willing to make to restore your balance?

What sacred whisper would you like to share with God today?

GOD, IS THIS LOVE?

In today's devotional moment with God, we unpack how the meaning of love has been redefined in our culture. The use of the word love was once sacred in our vocabulary. It was not used to describe our common affection for something or someone. Love was not used to describe our reaction to a pair of shoes, a beautiful house, a new car, or a movie we enjoyed. It was not used to describe an experience that we had with a group of friends but was an extraordinary emotion. In essence, the overuse of love as a description caused it to become common and ordinary.

When appropriately referenced as a defining moment, love is an intimate and deeply spiritual encounter with God. Love is how we as believers of the faith know and experience God. This is because love is the foundation of our relationship with God and should be the model for our relationships with others. What love does is create an experience of shared affection, acceptance, and belonging, and when these characteristic experiences are absent, then we should consult God in our sacred spaces and prayerfully whisper *God, is this love?*

> "Therefore, there is no greater love than the love of God, and God has affirmed this to us through Jesus Christ. This is why love must be the foundation."

The reality of love is that it should be the expectation for all relationships. God's expectation for us is that we love one another. We should expect that our human relationships have love as their foundation, because with love comes a mutual commitment to invest in the relationship, fight for the relationship, and maintain the relationship. God demonstrated to us what love should be and sacrificed His only son Jesus Christ for us. Jesus Christ's life was God's investment of love and His commitment to loving us. When God ransomed Jesus for our sins, this was God's willingness to maintain the relationship with us. There is no greater love than the love of God, and God has affirmed this to us through Jesus Christ. This is why love must be the foundation.

This is how God showed His love among us: He sent His one and only Son into the world that we might live through Him. This is love: not that we loved God, but that He loved us and sent His Son as an atoning sacrifice for our sins

1 John 4: 9-10

Prayer

Father God, give me the spiritual tenacity to handle existing and future relationships with love. God, give me wisdom so that I am unavailable to relationships that don't have Godly love as its foundation. This is my prayerful whisper. Amen.

Reflection

Invite God into this moment. Ask God to help you to discern whether your existing relationships have love as their foundation.

How will you handle relationships that you have discerned do not meet this criteria?

Do you have the courage to follow God's guidance in handling these relationships?

What sacred whisper would you like to share with God today?

GOD, LET ME NOT BE SEDUCED BY HATE

In today's devotional moment with God, we unpack the need to avoid being seduced by hate as a response to our own experiences of hurt. Hate is a sinful and intense emotion. It is actualized with words and actions that are angry, hostile, and belligerent. If there was ever a time any of us thought we hated someone, we have probably come to understand that what we defined as hate was nothing more than our temporary annoyance, frustration, or anger. The reason we can differentiate our past behaviors as not being comparable to hate is that our words and actions never exceeded our whispers to friends, murmurs under our breath, and an occasional side-eye. We never escalated or elevated our words or actions to cause harm to another human soul, nor did we cause permanent physical, emotional, or spiritual disability. In hindsight as mature Christians, we understand that even as insignificant as it may seem, our actions were inappropriate but did not rise to the level of hate. We understand that hate is a sin of the soul and can be seduced into action by the adversary. We understand that once hateful actions are taken against another person harm will be inflicted.

> "God did not create us with any of these deficiencies, but we were seduced by our environments and became products of them."

The truth about hate is that it is a learned behavior that is fueled by fear, insecurity, and jealousy. God did not create us with any of these deficiencies, but we were seduced by our environments and became products of them. Unfortunately, hate has seduced many people. This fiendish seduction has caused people to believe that those who are different are their enemies. Until people can see our differences as non-threatening, then the social order of our world is at risk. God has the power to free us from the seduction of hate. We can go to God in our sacred spaces and with true repentance prayerfully whisper, *God, let me not be seduced by hate.*

But I tell you, love your enemies and pray for those who per-secute you, that you may be children of your Father in heaven. He causes his sun to rise on the evil and the good and sends rain on the righteous and the unrighteous.

Matthew 5:44-45

Prayer

Father God, please teach me how to truly forgive those who have hurt, judged, and condemned me because of differences. God, show me what you desire for me to do to change their minds about me and you. This is my prayerful whisper. Amen.

Reflection

Invite God into this moment. What do you need God to do in your life as it relates to forgiveness?

How will you help others to understand that they should not fear differences and that hate is a sin of the soul?

What sacred whispers would you like to share with God today?

GOD, PROTECT ME WHEN I AM VULNERABLE

In today's devotional moment with God, we unpack the fear of being vulnerable. As believers, we understand that there are forces of darkness operating in our world and that we are prime targets for their spiritual attacks on our lives. Although we believe in the teachings of the Holy Bible and believe that God protects us, we still pray daily for our safety and for the safety of those we love. This is not because we don't trust or believe God, but because we don't trust the world in which we live. Experience has made us students of our world, and the world has taught us to avoid situations that will cause us to be in a vulnerable position.

In today's world, the vulnerable have predators. These predators use social media and technology to deceive, destroy, and launch spiritual attacks. Their tactics of kindness and helpfulness have been effective in conducting evil, and our evasive maneuvers have been ineffective in their cunningness. The unfortunate truth about being vulnerable in this world is that it is unavoidable. We will continue to be susceptible to predatorial attacks. However, there is safety in our sacred spaces, and it is where we access our war room to devise a defensive strategy with God. Then, when we have our battle-ready plans, we can ask for victory and prayerfully whisper, *God, protect me when I am vulnerable.*

> "We too must remember that God has the power to end our suffering, but He owes us no answer."

God does divinely intervene in our lives when we are most vulnerable to the attacks of our enemies. There are probably numerous divine interventions that happen daily without our awareness. Yet, when we are aware of these attacks, they are unforgettably painful. The story of Job in the bible gives the account of a righteous man who endured unmerited suffering and devastating loss. What Job desired most from God was an answer for his suffering. Job believed that his righteous walk had garnered favor with God. However, his long-suffering helped him to understand that God has no favorites. God eventually ended Job's suffering, but God owed Job no answer for it. We too must remember that God has the power to end our suffering, but He owes us no answer.

At this, Job got up and tore his robe, and shaved his head. Then he fell to the ground in worship and said: "Naked I came from my mother's womb, and naked I will depart. The Lord gave and the Lord has taken away; may the name of the Lord be praised." In all this, Job did not sin by charging God with wrongdoing.

Job 1:20-22

Prayer

Father God, I pray for the strength to endure times of suffering. God, please help me to not blame you and be so angry that I cannot connect with you spiritually and emotionally. God, soothe my soul and anchor me in worship. Fill my mouth with praise. This is my prayerful whisper. Amen.

Reflection

Invite God into this moment. What problems if any do you see with the response of Job to God?

How do you respond to unwarranted suffering in your own life?

What sacred whisper would you like to share with God today?

GOD, I AM NOT A VICTIM ANYMORE

In today's devotional moment with God, we unpack how to reconcile the label of victim. If we have ever participated in team-building activities at our place of employment, at school, or with an organization, then we were probably asked to introduce ourselves in a few sentences. We may have been asked to tell the group something about ourselves that we would not mind everyone knowing. By the time the exercise of brief introductions had concluded, we had safely taken our seats among the group. No one questioned what we shared or didn't share, and our carefully worded answers were well received because they had no depth into our personal lives. They were only surface details meant to keep the meeting space safe and comfortable. Even though all eyes were on us during these moments of introduction, no one noticed our nervousness. We had survived. Even with this opportunity to tell our story of survival, we had determined that it was not a safe space. These unsuspecting friendly faces knew nothing about the challenges we had to endure to rid ourselves of the label of victim, and that day was not the moment for full disclosure. For survivors, these common life experiences remind us that there is a need for us all to have a sacred space to connect with God so that we can process and prayerfully whisper, *God, I am not a victim anymore.*

> "The pain did not make Jesus a victim, and it does not make us a victim either. An authentic and real emotional response to pain should be a human response. This is because if it was good enough for Jesus, shouldn't it be good enough for us too?"

Some people have survived unimaginable situations and have never chosen to share their stories. The unfortunate truth is that we exist in a culture that prefers that we project strength in the face of adversity. We have become so good at pretending to be strong that our responses to trauma and pain are to apologize and express sympathy for victims. The inadequacy of these responses to pain is a stark contrast to the tears of Jesus. Jesus wept at the tomb of his friend Lazarus, not because He was powerless to change things, but because He experienced the pain. The pain did not make Jesus a victim, and it does not make us a victim either. An authentic and real emotional response to pain should always be a human response. This is because if it was good enough for Jesus, shouldn't it be enough for us too? Survivors don't need our permission to emote or tell their stories, and this should never be an expectation. But giving people the space to experience real emotions is an expectation and an act of human compassion.

Jesus wept. Then the Jews said, "See how He loved him!"

John 11:35-36

Prayer

Father God, help me to be aware of those in my peer circles who need an authentic sounding board, and an attentive listening ear. God, help me to provide compassion in the midst of pain. This is my prayerful whisper. Amen.

Reflection

Invite God into this moment. What can you do to support those who have survived painful experiences?

Is it possible for you to respond authentically without fear?

What do you fear about others' pain?

What sacred whisper would you like to share with God today?

GOD, ADMONISH WHAT IS VENGEFUL

In today's devotional moment with God, we unpack why we harbor grievances to the point of becoming vengeful. Arguments and disagreements are natural in most relationships. When spouses or lifetime friends reflect on their years together, it is almost unbelievable to hear that they have never argued or disagreed about anything. Confessions like these can make some of us feel guilty that we lacked the discipline to be in this group of successful communicators. Nevertheless, when our relationships are burdened by arguments and disagreements, we will usually make a conscious effort to avoid conflict and reconcile by seeking forgiveness. The reason we do this is because we understand that arguments and disagreements can cause a person to experience emotional pain, especially when harsh words are exchanged.

Harsh words have a way of being received far worse than they were intended to be and can trigger a range of emotional responses. This is why we should be careful in how we engage people during an argument or disagreement because our behaviors have consequences.

> "Vengeance will always be the exclusive right of God, and only He has the authority to determine when it is justified."

When we are hurt and our painful emotions are unresolved, then there is a greater possibility for us to become vengeful. Vengefulness happens when we escalate our painful feelings to acts of retaliation. Although this may seem like something we would never consider as a Christian, pain and anger can cause anyone to fall under the influence of the devil and pursue vengeance.

What we need to always remember is that vengeance is under the sole authority of God. Vengeance will always be God's exclusive right, and only He has the authority to determine when it is justified. Whenever our emotions escalate to being unreasonable and unwise, this is when we should step into our sacred spaces, seek the Holy Spirit, pray fervently, and prayerfully whisper, *God, admonish what is vengeful.*

Do not take revenge, my dear friends, but leave room for God's wrath, for it is written: "It is mine to avenge; I will repay," says the Lord.

Romans 12:19

Prayer

Father God, I pray that the Holy Spirit will guide and teach me how to deal with disagreements, and harsh words that have been spoken to me so that I will not become vengeful. This is my prayerful whisper. Amen.

Reflection

Invite God into this moment. Are you managing arguments and disagreements with the grace that God has given to each of us?

How can you address hurt feelings and painful words so they do not become acts of vengeance?

What sacred whisper would you like to share with God today?

GOD, PREPARE ME FOR THE HARVEST

In today's devotional moment with God, we unpack how to manage the presence of God's favor with grace. We have probably all been recipients and witnesses to divinely designated harvest seasons. Some of these harvest seasons were ours, while others were not. This does not mean that we were in a season of famine, but to point out that God blesses us daily. Still, some seasons are more plentiful than others. Divinely designated harvest seasons are when we as members of the family of God reap an abundance of blessings. For example, when everything in our personal, professional, and spiritual lives is working well without faltering, this is the blessing of a harvest season. When we are excelling and exceeding at everything we do, this is the blessing of a harvest season. When our prayers and petitions are answered seemingly without delay, this is the blessing of a harvest season. All of these experiences are associated with being a benefactor of a divinely designated harvest season.

However, when others are in the midst of a harvest season but we are not, then we need to be careful to not allow feelings of jealousy to take root in our lives. One of the first human responses to jealousy is denial. But when we have begun to complain to God and accuse Him of forgetting or skipping over our season, then we have become jealous. As a result, we raised comparisons and complaints simply because it was not our season. We were convinced that because our works of service for the kingdom were significant, this made us God's favorite. And just like we were not happy about somebody else's harvest season, there are people who will not be happy about our season either.

> "Divinely designated harvest seasons are when we as members of the family of God reap an abundance of blessings."

Jealous and envious people can behave sinfully towards us and God. They will revel in opportunities to disrupt our harvest seasons and will consistently challenge whether we are the rightful benefactor. They will attempt to stand in the room in our designated spots and sit at the table in our designated seats. Although they will be unsuccessful, it will not prevent them from being a disruptor.

Before we assume a posture of jealousy or envy and become a disruptor, we need to prayerfully pause and shift our focus to our spiritual preparation. We need to ask ourselves if we are ready for the harvest that God has prepared for us and if we are capable of being good stewards of it. God expects that what He provides will yield an increase, not just for the recipient but for the body of believers.

In our sacred spaces, let us begin to connect with God before our divinely designated harvest season arrives, and prayerfully whisper, *God prepare me for the harvest.*

What causes fights and quarrels among you? Don't they come from your desires that battle within you? You desire but do not have, so you kill. You covet but you cannot get what you want, so you quarrel and fight. You do not have because you do not ask God.

James 4:1-2

Prayer

Father God, I admit that there are times I am envious and jealous when it is not my harvest season. God, help me to be patient as I wait for you to prepare me for your season of favor for my life. This is my prayerful whisper. Amen.

Reflection

Invite God into this moment. Are you coveting someone else's favor?

What do you need to do to be ready to handle the costs of God's favor in your own life?

What sacred whisper would you like to share with God today?

GOD, KEEP ME FROM TEMPTATIONS

In today's devotional moment with God, we unpack the challenge of resisting temptations. Living a life of salvation is complicated when there is this constant battle to resist every temptation we encounter daily. The Christian lifestyle is hard work. We have to strategically avoid and evade the traps set by the adversary to entice us to sin. We will need to strategically use the power of our will and the consciousness of our conviction to serve God with reverence and obedience. This means we must hate no one, love everyone, and ignore every temptation to take revenge on those who have caused us harm. This is just a brief synopsis of what it takes to maintain a Christian lifestyle.

> "At the core of temptation is our sinful desire for something that we believe will satisfy us in some way."

At the core of temptation is our sinful desire for something that we believe will satisfy us in some way. Oftentimes temptations are desires that we have suppressed for a long time, but this is what makes them more susceptible to trigger events. This is why when we begin to experience moments of temptation, and the pressure increases, we should use our sacred spaces to shelter with God. Then as we prepare to resist the adversary's pressure campaign, we will have the clarity to prayerfully whisper, *God, keep me from temptations.*

Jesus in His human experience was tempted by the devil with bread and power after a forty-day fast. Yet, Jesus resisted the temptation because He knew that power does not come from the powerless. If we are to resist temptation, we must take our cues from Jesus, and understand that the one who can fulfill the desires of our hearts is God alone.

Take delight in the Lord, and he will give you the desires of your heart.

Psalm 37:4

Prayer

Father God, help me to overcome moments when I am tempted by wrong choices and want to satisfy myself and my ego. God, be my guide and my fortress so that I can continue to live in obedience to you. This is my prayerful whisper. Amen.

Reflection

Invite God into this moment. What temptations are you struggling with at this time in your life?

How will you maintain a Christian lifestyle and identity when facing temptations?

What sacred whisper do you want to share with God today?

PART III: CONVERSATION

COMMENCING CONVERSATION THROUGH SACRED WHISPERS

GOD, HERE I AM

In today's devotional moment with God, we reflect on the conversation between God and Moses. Moses' story illustrates to us how to handle the divine assignments that impact our lives. The story of Moses in the bible begins with his mother Jochebed, who in an act of desperation, placed her infant in a tar and pitch-coated papyrus basket and set it afloat on the Nile River. This bold and courageous action was taken to protect her child from the genocide of his generation. This is because the Pharaoh of Egypt had ordered the death of every newborn Hebrew male. But Moses escaped death when he was drawn from the water by Pharaoh's daughter and became her son.

As a Prince of Egypt, Moses learned to revere and reverence the power of Pharaoh. He had sworn to protect the Egyptian dynasty from all threats, whether foreign or domestic. At this time in Moses' life, the Hebrew people were slaves in Egypt. They were subjected to extreme brutality and were worked to excruciating fatigue. Moses was overseeing Pharoah's interests among the slaves when he saw an Egyptian slave master brutally beating a Hebrew slave. Moses intervened and killed the slave master, but when Pharoah learned of the death, Moses was forced to flee Egypt into the wilderness of Midian.

The fugitive Moses was shepherding his father-in-law's flock in Midian when he saw what appeared to be a burning bush. Moses was curious and wanted to understand why the bush did not burn to ash. So he climbed the mountain of God for an answer. In a theophanic encounter, Moses was given the revelation of his divine assignment. God instructed Moses to return to Egypt and liberate the Hebrew slaves from their bondage. Moses was to become God's deliverer for the Hebrew people.

> "In today's Christian life, we don't have to look for God on mountaintops or in cool garden breezes or in a pillar of fire. This is because Jesus sacrificed His life for us, and by grace made it possible for us to have direct access to God for intimate conversations."

Although Moses had not asked God for guidance, prayed to God for wisdom, or waited for God to resolve his predicament, he heard God speak his divine assignment into existence. Moses' conversation with God was a supernatural event with significant benefits for him and the Hebrew people. The takeaway for us today is that conversations with God continue to provide benefits and blessings. We can thank Jesus because His sacrifice made it possible for us to have direct access to God for intimate conversations about everything. Therefore, as we pray and converse with God in our sacred spaces, let us avail ourselves to divinely orchestrated assignments and prayerfully whisper, *God, here I am.*

When the Lord saw that he had gone over to look, God called to him from within the bush, "Moses! Moses! And Moses said, "Here I am." "Do not come any closer," God said. "Take off your sandals, for the place where you are standing is holy ground."

Exodus 3:5

Prayer

Father God, thank you for speaking directly to me, and for allowing me to hear your divine plans for my life. God, I am grateful that you provide opportunities for me to be an echo of your voice in the world for the benefit of your people. This is my prayerful whisper. Amen.

Reflection

Invite God into this moment. What conversation do you need to begin with God today?

What is happening in your life that needs clarity?

What sacred whisper would you like to share with God today?

GOD, THANK YOU FOR THE ANSWERED PRAYER

In today's devotional moment with God, we revisit the very familiar story of Zechariah and the conversation with God's messenger. Zechariah's story illustrates to us that God is always listening and never forgets our prayers, even if we do. Zechariah was a priest from the order of Abijah. This was his life, and he had vowed to serve God faithfully with reverence and obedience.

Zechariah believed that he would have one wife and father no children. This is because it appeared that God had not answered his prayers, and he remained childless. This was the fate he had accepted, and as a result, he no longer prayed for an heir of his name. Nonetheless, Zechariah never wavered in his service and according to his call, he stood before the altar of the Lord and prayed not for himself, but for the people to have the answers to their prayers. Then, the unexpected happened. God's Angel Gabriel appeared to him at the altar and announced that his prayers for a child had been answered. Skeptically, Zechariah laughed because duty had blinded him to God's divine timing.

> "God never forgets our prayer, even if we do."

Zechariah's encounter demonstrates some important lessons on the value of faithful prayers. The first is that God never forgets our prayers, even if we do. Oftentimes, we believe that when God has not given us an immediate answer, then His silence means 'no.' A delayed answer to our prayer does not mean that God has denied the request. God may have delayed giving us an answer not because we are unworthy, but because we are not ready. Although this perspective may be difficult to accept, God knows our capacity to handle what He provides in every season of our lives. Secondly, we must be ready to receive the answer to our prayers. Everyone outside of the temple who was praying was expecting an answer from God, except Zechariah. His focus was clearly on his priestly duties. We must be careful not to become so duty-bound in our prayers and worship, that we are unprepared to receive the answer God has for us. The takeaway is our prayers must be driven by faith and not just duty. The good news is that we can continue to work through the challenges of our unanswered prayers in our sacred spaces with God. We should always expect God to answer our prayers, and with faith prayerfully whisper, *God, thank you for the answered prayer.*

But the angel said to him: "Do not be afraid, Zechariah; your prayer has been heard. Your wife Elizabeth will bear you a son, and you are to call him John.
Luke 1:13

Prayer

Father God, teach me to always expect answers to my prayers, and not decide that a delay is a denial. God, teach me to be patient and to persevere in my season of waiting. This is my prayerful whisper. Amen.

Reflection

Invite God into this moment. What unanswered prayers have you declared to be your fate?

What prayers have you stopped praying but need to resume so that you can hear God's answer?

What sacred whisper would you like to share with God today?

GOD, FORGIVE ME

In today's devotional moment with God, we reflect on one of the last conversations David had with God during an inspired moment. David's conversation with God illustrates to us how God handles our confessions with love and forgiveness. Similar to some of us, King David leaned towards cover-ups instead of confessions. The man who had defeated armies and danced before God had one last opportunity, and in a moment of full disclosure, he confessed. David knew that he was imperfect and flawed. He knew he had ignored and disregarded the laws of Moses. He knew he had given in to his desires of passion and power and failed the tests of temptation. More importantly, David knew that a consequence for his sins was inevitable. To lessen the impact, he worshiped and repented in a way that pleased God. With the skill of a masterful musician, David worshiped at the seat of God. He knew that adoration was a key to God's heart and that great screw-ups required awesome worship. David's private confessions given in his sacred spaces with God turned to praise and worship, and into prayerful whispers that if summarized would be, *God, forgive me.*

> "Our conversations with God are not just for our lists of asks. Instead, our conversations are opportunities to confess, repent, and worship in a spirit of truth and transparency."

If we are to take a page from David's playbook, then we must learn that our conversations with God are not just for our lists of asks. Instead, our conversations are opportunities to confess, repent, and worship in a spirit of truth and transparency. This is how David became a man after God's own heart. Let us learn from David by following his example and unburden ourselves from the sins that bind us.

"If my house were not right with God, surely, he would not have made with me an everlasting covenant, arranged and secured in every part; surely, he would not bring to fruition my salvation and grant me my every desire."

2 Samuel 23:5

Prayer

Father God, teach me to live a life of transparency and truth so that I can become unburdened with the secrecy of my sins. This is my prayerful whisper. Amen.

Reflection

Invite God into this moment. What do you need to confess to God?

What secrets and sins are holding you captive and are keeping you separated from God?

What sacred whispers would you like to share with God today?

GOD, MY LIFE IS IN YOUR HANDS

In today's devotional moment with God, we reflect on an unusual conversation between God and the Prophet Jeremiah. Jeremiah's story illustrates to us how to follow God's instruction, even when it doesn't make sense.

Jeremiah was an anointed prophet of God. He had the difficult task of echoing God's wisdom, warnings, and impending wrath to King Zedekiah, and to the people in Judah. Jeremiah was despised by the people for his prophecies. This is because no one wanted to hear that they would be defeated and devastated for their wrongdoings, or that God's wrath was inevitable. Their denial felt safer. Yet, Jeremiah continued to prophesy anyway, and this resulted in him being imprisoned to silence him. What the king did not understand was that it was impossible to silence the voice of God. Not only did God continue to speak through Jeremiah, but God gave him specific instructions. In the midst of an impending enemy occupation and exile, God instructed Jeremiah to purchase the land of his relatives. A confused Jeremiah acquired the land but wanted to know why. This is because, from his natural lens, the land would soon be occupied, destroyed, and worthless. God responded to Jeremiah and affirmed His instructions, not as an explanation, but as an affirmation.

> "It is important that we as Christians remain faithful and obedient to God, especially when we cannot see the value or understand the purpose."

Not everything God does makes sense to us at the moment. We have probably all had experiences where God instructed us to do something that made no sense to us. And like Jeremiah, we questioned the reason God gave us this instruction because we could not see any value in it. We may have even questioned if the instruction was a test of our faith or a trick of the adversary. Whatever conclusion we may have reached, our follow-through was based on our faith in God. This is why it is important that we as Christians remain faithful and obedient to God, especially when we cannot see the value or understand the purpose.

The true nugget of Jeremiah's story is that we must learn to trust the plans of God which are perfect in every season of our lives. Then, communicate with God in our sacred spaces, and reconcile what we don't understand with prayerful whispers, *God, my life is in your hands.*

Then the word of the Lord came to Jeremiah: "I am the Lord, the God of all mankind. Is anything too hard for me?"

Jeremiah 32:26-27

Prayer

Father God, I pray that I have the faith and obedience to follow your instructions, even when it doesn't make sense in the natural world. God, may I always be mindful that you are the God of all of creation and nothing is too hard for you. God, may I find peace in knowing that my life is in your hands. This is my prayerful whisper. Amen.

Reflection

Invite God into this moment. Do you have people in your life who want to silence you because you follow God's instructions according to His Word in scripture?

How does God want you to respond?

What sacred whisper would you like to share with God today?

GOD, THIS ASSIGNMENT IS CHALLENGING

In today's devotional moment with God, we reflect on the test of Abraham, and the faith he used to converse wisely and reverently with God. Abraham's story illustrates to us that God does not need our permission to test our faith with challenging assignments. Abraham had no issues faithfully obeying God, but he was to be tested.

Abraham had completed every divine assignment, and now the ultimate test was before him. God directed him to sacrifice his long-awaited son Isaac. This was a big ask! However, Abraham believed that his obedience was more valuable to God than any personal sacrifice he could make. He had become accustomed to the personal sacrifices and challenges of obeying God, and many of these challenges preceded the birth of Isaac. At God's command, he had left his family and all those he loved and knew in Ur, and traveled to an unspecified distant land that God was going to eventually reveal to him. He had encountered kings and armies known for their treachery and survived. He had disguised his wife as his sister to preserve their lives and secure their safe passage. He had intervened in God's plan to destroy Sodom and Gomorrah to save Lot and his family. Abraham had sent away his son Ishmael to protect him. He did all of this to complete the divine assignments God had given to him. Faith was something that Abraham understood and embraced, but obedience was his personal choice.

> "It is important that we rely on our faith to provide us with the courage and capacity to complete whatever divine test or assignment God has for us."

It would be safe to say that no one could imagine the range of emotions that Abraham must have felt when God directed him to sacrifice his son. The anxiety, fear, anger, or grief that must have gripped him in the moment was unimaginable. Abraham's test of faith and obedience was about trusting God with what he valued most in life, but the decision to endure the testing itself was always his choice.

We handle testing assignments and decisions in our sacred spaces with God first. With God, we can process the purpose of our testing, and then in a prayerful whisper acknowledge, *God, this assignment is challenging.*

In the Christian life, we will encounter difficult periods of testing. It is important that we rely on our faith to provide us with the courage and capacity to complete whatever divine test or assignment God has for us. This is why the lesson of Abraham's story is to be mindful that God does not need a reason to test our faithfulness or obedience because both will always be our personal choice.

Sometime *later God tested Abraham. He said to him,* *"Abraham!" "Here I am," he replied. Then God said, "Take your* *son, your only son, whom you love—Isaac—and go to the region* *of Moriah. Sacrifice him there as a burnt offering on a moun-* *tain I will show you."*

Genesis 22:1-2

Prayer

Father God, please provide me with the faith and courage to *handle periods of divine testing with obedience. This is my* *prayerful whisper. Amen.*

Reflection

Invite God into this moment. Do you think that you are capable of handling the testing of your faith and obedience?

Based on your understanding of who God is to you, how will you handle the challenges of obedience in a difficult assignment?

What sacred whisper would you like to share with God today?

GOD, MAKE ME A WORTHY CHOICE

In today's devotional moment with God, we revisit a conversation between God and Samuel, who was both a judge and prophet of Israel. Samuel's story illustrates to us how God will transform and equip those He has chosen.

Samuel was distraught after hearing the Israelites had rejected God as their sovereign. The Israelites wanted to be ruled by an earthly king. Their demand for a king was caused by their desire to be like other earthly kingdoms who were ruled by men, and who appeared strong, strategic, and courageous to other nations. God responded to their demand by instructing Samuel to give the people what they wanted. And so God chose Saul as Israel's first king.

This is the part in the story that still has spiritual revelation for us today. Once God chose Saul as Israel's king, he experienced a supernatural transformation. The Bible records that Saul became a different man. Although he had the stature of an earthly king and appeared to be comparable to their might, he was different because he had been endowed with the anointed spirit of God. It was God's spirit that set Saul apart from any other king. As a result, he was given the authority to stand as the face of God before the people.

"God will transform our hearts so that we are spiritually equipped for the assignments that lie ahead."

When God chooses us for any earthly assignment there will be a period of preparation and transformation. God will transform our hearts so that we are spiritually equipped for the assignments that lie ahead. This is the reason we should not be ambivalent in acknowledging God as the transformational source of people's lives. Every day we witness people doing extraordinary things that impact our world for the greater good. Many of them would agree that their achievements were God-orchestrated. They believe by faith that their wisdom, ability, and success are a direct result of God's spirit within them. This is why every conversational moment with God is an opportunity to connect with Him in our sacred spaces and to be open to His transforming spirit that sets us apart. As we pray, let our prayerful whispers include, *God, make me a worthy choice.*

"Samuel said to all the people, "Do you see the man the Lord has chosen? There is no one like him among all the people."

1 Samuel 10:24

Prayer

Father God, I pray that you will transform me for every assignment you have ordained for me in this life. God, prepare me for the periods of preparation and transformation so that I am a worthy choice. This is my prayerful whisper. Amen.

Reflection

Invite God into this moment. Do you believe that God is still transforming people's lives with His spirit?

What evidence do you see in your own life or in someone else's?

Do you believe you are or could be a worthy choice?

What sacred whisper would you like to share with God today?

GOD, YOU KNOW
US ALL

In today's devotional moment with God, we reflect on a conversation between God and the Apostle Peter. Peter's story illustrates to us that we need to be open to the message and messengers of God regardless of appearance, cultural or ethnic affiliation.

After Jesus' ascension, Peter struggled in the early days of his ministry. His struggle was primarily with the Gentiles because he was not convinced that salvation had come to them. At the center of his struggle was a gentile named Cornelius. Cornelius was a God-fearing man residing in Caesarea. He was kind to the poor even though he was a centurion in the Italian regiment. As directed by the Lord's angel, Cornelius sent men under his authority to Peter requesting his presence in Caesarea. When Peter arrived, he was greeted with a reverence reserved for God's Prophets. What a moment! Peter was standing in the midst of a community of believing Gentiles. With all of the excitement captured in scripture around Peter's presence, we often miss his reaction to the Gentiles. Peter had no offense or hesitancy because it was undeniable that the Holy Spirit was upon this group of believing Gentiles. At that moment, Peter himself was convicted about the salvation of the Gentiles, and it was just as Jesus had said when He was with him.

> "When we have a revelation of God's intentions,
> then we will humbly pray with sacred whispers that
> affirm, God, you know us all."

Consider the number of times God may have sent a word to us by way of a messenger. Unfortunately, we may have been hesitant to respond to the messenger because of their appearance, and cultural or ethnic affiliation. Too often we have questioned whether God has deemed certain people groups worthy of His salvation. We assume that we are worthy because we are not them, but we assume in vain. This is because God has no favorites!

The point of this story is that the blood sacrifice of Jesus Christ redeemed and reconciled *all* to God. This may all sound a little preachy, but at some point, we need to step into our sacred spaces and examine ourselves. When we have a revelation of God's intentions, then we will humbly pray with sacred whispers that affirm, *God, you know us all.* Like Peter, we should be ready to respond to the message and whoever the messengers might be in the moment.

Then Peter began to speak: "I now realize how true it is that God does not show favoritism but accepts from every nation the one who fears him and does what is right.

Acts 10:34-35

Prayer

Father God, help me with any offense I may have with people who are different. God, please humble me so that I always have clarity and confirmation about your people and your kingdom. This is my prayerful whisper. Amen.

Reflection

Invite God into this moment. Who has God sent to you with a message, and you were hesitant?

What will it take for you to believe that God has no favorites?

Do you need to change your response to messengers who may offend you? Just know God is waiting to help.

What sacred whisper would you like to share with God today?

GOD, I'VE COMPLAINED ENOUGH

In today's devotional moment with God, we reflect on the story of Job, and his lament for an answer that ultimately led to a difficult conversation with God. Job's story illustrates to us that no complaint against God for His decisions is valid. This is because we cannot know or wrap our human minds around the thoughts of a supreme being who is God.

Job was a faithful man in awe of God, who consistently rejected evil. As such, God favored him. This was until the day when the angels gathered before God, and satan came to look for someone to devour. God presented Job as a candidate for testing, but with the one condition that his life remained untouched. With the permission of God, satan inflicted a reign of devastation, and Job lost everything that God had provided. Everything means his wife, children, friends, land, livestock, health, and all of his earthly possessions. Covered in boils and blisters, Job lamented and asked God to explain why his life lay in ruin. By the time Job had finished his last lament, he had spent countless hours, days, and even months complaining about the injustices inflicted upon him. Job had never considered the sound of God's response in his ears. But when Job heard God's voice speaking to him, the bible describes this theophanic experience as a tornadic-like wind encircling him. He must have been terrified when he heard the cacophonous roar of an invisible stampede. He must have shaken when the thunderous voice demanded that he identify who had given him the authority to question God's decisions. If there was ever a moment where it was possible to escape the presence of God, this would have been it. Job realized that God had spoken, and quickly repented for his arrogance and haughtiness.

> "Our sacred spaces provide us with the safety to process the meaning of God-permitted tests. This is so we can pray for clarity, address our spirit of complaint, and then prayerfully whisper to God, I've complained enough."

We have all had seasons in our lives when things were just terrible. Although we may have made every effort to fix what was broken and resolve problems that created chaos, we were simply unsuccessful. We may have even complained to God about how unfair life was despite our relationship with Him. The truth is that seasons of devastation are extremely difficult. Nevertheless, our sacred spaces provide us with the safety to process the meaning of God-permitted tests. This is so we can pray for clarity, and address our spirit of complaint, and then prayerfully whisper to *God, I've complained enough.*

"Then Job replied to the Lord: "I know that you can do all things; no purpose of yours can be thwarted."
Job 42:1-2

Prayer

Father God, teach me how to pray more and complain less. God, I pray that you will guide me with your wisdom and give me the discernment to know when I need to confess and repent so that I am always reconciled to you. This is my prayerful whisper. Amen.

Reflection

Invite God into this moment. What will you do to change your behavior of complaint towards God and others?

Do you think that spending time with God gives you increased clarity about His plans for you?

What did you learn from Job's story?

What sacred whisper would you like to share with God today?

GOD, GIVE ME
WHAT I NEED

In today's devotional moment with God, we reflect on the conversation between God and Moses on a mountaintop. Moses' story illustrates to us that God knows who we are and what we are capable of accomplishing, even when it is not evident to us.

The clip note version of Moses' story was that he had attempted to explain to God why he was not qualified to be His spokesman. When God assigned Moses the responsibility of negotiating the release of the Hebrew slaves from Egypt, he stated every excuse, weakness, and impairment that he could think of to indicate that he wasn't qualified for the assignment. Standing before God, Moses rejected the responsibility of leading God's people. This was not solely because he believed he wasn't qualified, but because he was afraid. Moses was afraid to stand before Pharaoh as a powerless man who knew he could not defeat Pharaoh's iron-clad chariots or experienced battle-ready army.

Moreover, Moses knew that he had a credibility problem with the Hebrews. This is because they knew his history. They knew that Moses had been raised in Pharaoh's house as a Prince of Egypt, and his past still plagued his present mindset. As such, Moses pleaded with God to choose someone else. But

God had a plan to free the people, and Moses was to be their liberator.

The jewel of today's lesson is that God's Word will never return void of its purpose. This is why God instructed Moses to take his shepherd's staff and cloak and use them as a sign of His omnipotence. The man Moses was not given chariots or armies or tools of war, but was given something more powerful, and that is God's Word. On the Word of God, he would prevail and be victorious against a contender who was larger, stronger, and faster, because God was with him.

> "Regardless of what stalled us, we need to remember Moses' story. This is because it amplifies God, who is bigger than the hardest assignments in our lives."

Take a moment. Now reflect on those times when we didn't want to do the hard stuff. We were certain that we weren't the right person for the assignment at the time. Maybe we told ourselves, that we needed to get more education, training, or experience. Maybe we told ourselves, that we didn't have a full picture of all the details that needed to be tackled to be successful. Maybe we were afraid of failing, and feared being subjected to the humiliation of our peers, friends, or even family members with their *I told you so*. Regardless of what stalled us, we need to remember Moses' story. This is because it amplifies God, who is bigger than the hardest assignments in our lives. Therefore, we can take refuge in our sacred spaces and be assured that God is with us and has us covered. When God has given us His Word, we can prayerfully whisper, *God, give me what I need.*

And God said, "I will be with you. And this will be the sign to you that it is I who have sent you: When you have brought the people out of Egypt, you will worship God on this mountain."

Exodus 3:12

Prayer

Father God, I pray that I will learn to trust you while tackling the hard assignments. God, assure me of your Word so that I will be successful. This is my prayerful whisper. Amen.

Reflection

Invite God into this moment. What thoughts or feelings are causing you to make excuses for not tackling the hard assignments in your life?

Based on Moses' story, what role will your faith have when it comes to making decisions about the hard assignments and moving forward?

What sacred whispers would you like to share with God today?

GOD, I NEED A MIRACULOUS MOMENT

In today's devotional moment with God, we reflect on the conversation between Jesus and some of the Apostles. Jesus illustrates to us that we should not doubt our faith or preparation.

After hearing the instructions of the man standing on the shore, the Apostle John recognized His words as those of Jesus. The Apostles had scattered after His death and resurrection and were lost without Him. They could not seem to figure out what to do and to make matters worse, there were still sizable crowds following them. For three years, Jesus taught the Apostles how to handle hunger, sickness, demons, and so much more. Despite all of their spiritual training, they seemed confused about how to minister to the people. Jesus had not only performed multiple miracles in their presence but had repeatedly emphasized trusting the power of their faith.

In a memory-triggering moment, Jesus directed them to cast their fishing nets to the right side of the boat. The familiarity of the moment reminded them of their calling to follow Jesus, and of the assignment to bring the gospel to the world. As they returned to shore, Jesus invited them to bring some of their fish, and all of their faith to the meal. When we are feeling defeated and exhausted and are ready to give up because we don't know what to do, Jesus will remind us of our calling and invite us to bring our faith to the moment.

> "When we are feeling defeated and exhausted and are ready to give up because we don't know what to do, Jesus will remind us of our calling and invite us to bring our faith to the moment."

We can probably all identify with the Apostles and recall times in our own lives when we were feeling defeated and just wanted to give up. There was no one there to encourage us or remind us of our faith, but we mustered enough spiritual stamina to believe that God could work things out. Then in a prayerful whisper we uttered, *God, I need a miraculous moment.*

Today, we are still living and breathing witnesses of Jesus, and what is possible with faith. We just have to remember that our sacred spaces are where we converse with God about our ministry and mission, and the miracles we need to complete our assignments.

"When they landed, they saw a fire of burning coals there with fish on it, and some bread. Jesus said to them, "Bring some of the fish you have just caught." So Simon Peter climbed back into the boat and dragged the net ashore. It was full of large fish, 153, but even with so many the net was not torn."
John 21:9-11

Prayer

Father God, I pray that you will give me daily reminders of my faith and what is possible with you. God, give me the spiritual stamina to defeat frustration and exhaustion with the assignments you have entrusted to me. This is my prayerful whisper. Amen.

Reflection

Invite God into this moment. Have you had difficulty recognizing Jesus in moments when you feel frustrated and defeated?

What reminders do you need about your faith in God to move past these thoughts and feelings?

What sacred whisper would you like to share with God today?

GOD, WRESTLE
WITH ME

In today's devotional moment with God, we revisit the story of Jacob who the bible records wrestled with God. Jacob's story illustrates to us that wrestling with God over difficult decisions has spiritual benefits.

Following God's directive, Jacob left the house of Laban where he had hidden for 20 years, and began the difficult journey home to Canaan. The reason Jacob had left his country and hidden was because he had willfully stolen his twin brother Esau's birthright blessing and fled. Jacob knew that Esau was entitled to justice, and there was no moratorium that would keep him from enduring the consequences of his actions. In those 20 years of hiding, he had married Leah and Rachel, fathered children, and obtained wealth. When Jacob's servitude arrangement ended, he made the difficult decision to return to the land of his father and face his brother, and the consequences he had long feared. This was the reason Jacob wrestled with God. He wrestled with God for a blessing that would banish the consequences of his sin, and his debt to Esau, and provide a divine intervention that would spare his life.

"There will be times in our lives when we will wrestle with God because we have difficult decisions that will need divine interventions."

There will be times in our lives when we will wrestle with God because we have difficult decisions that will need divine interventions. God is the source of divine interventions and lifesaving blessings. He establishes the course for us to overcome. This is the spiritual benefit of wrestling with God. This is why when we are anxious and fearful of facing the consequences of our actions, that we should meet with God in our sacred spaces, and wrestle through the process of overcoming. In our moments alone with God, let our prayerful whisper be, *God, wrestle with me.*

The man asked him, "What is your name?" "Jacob," he answered. Then the man said, "Your name will no longer be Jacob, but Israel because you have struggled with God and with humans and have overcome."

Genesis 32:27-28

Prayer

Father God, please help me recognize when I need to wrestle with you about difficult decisions that need divine interventions. God, help me to not allow fear to keep me from advancing my future hopes because I fear past mistakes. This is my prayerful whisper. Amen.

Reflection

Invite God into this moment. Have you ever wrestled with God to be reconciled in your life?

What do you need to wrestle with God about to move forward with your pursuits and purpose?

What sacred whisper would you like to share with God today?

GOD, I'M THANKFUL YOU HEAR ME

In today's devotional moment with God, we reflect on Hagar's wilderness experience, and how it provoked her to cry out to God. Hagar's story illustrates that God hears us and is willing to respond because of His grace, mercy, and love for us.

Hagar was an Egyptian slave, and her master was Sarah who was the wife of Abraham. As a slave, she had no rights, no choices, and no voice. The expectation was that she be completely obedient. As such, Hagar bore a son named Ishmael because Sarah had commanded it. Ishmael was the first-born son of Abraham and was conceived to force God's promise to manifest. God had promised Abraham that he would father an heir who would produce a great nation that would outnumber the stars. But he fathered a child prematurely because of the influence of his wife Sarah.

Ishmael's birth initially pleased Sarah until God opened her womb, and she birthed Isaac. Sarah wanted there to be no competition between Ishmael and Isaac. So the child Ishmael and his mother Hagar were banished to the wilderness. There they wandered until their supply of water was gone. Resolved to die, Hagar cried out to the God of Abraham to spare her child's life.

In response to her cries, an Angel of the Lord appeared and guided her to a well to draw water to save their lives.

> "What we should take away from Hagar's conversation with God is that crying out to God gets His attention. This is because God is always responsive to the cries of His creation."

Whatever joy or privilege Hagar may have experienced with the birth of Ishmael, it was short-lived. She and her son could never be more than slaves to their owners. Hagar was an Egyptian, and she knew enough to cry out to the God of Abraham to save her son. How she came to know God remains a mystery. But it is possible that her proximity to Abraham was enough for the moment.

Some of today's readers or listeners may not know God as intimately as they would like. But what we should take away from Hagar's conversation with God is that crying out to God gets His attention. This is because God is always responsive to the cries of His creation. If there is ever a time when we are desperate to hear God speak to us, remember that our sacred spaces are reserved for moments like these, and we too can cry out with prayerful whispers of *God, I'm thankful you hear me.*

"God heard the boy crying, and the angel of God called to Hagar from heaven and said to her, "What is the matter, Hagar? Do not be afraid; God has heard the boy crying as he lies there. Lift the boy and take him by the hand, for I will make him into a great nation."

Genesis 21:17-18

Prayer

Father God, thank you for hearing my cry and answering me. God, I am grateful that you are never outside of my reach, and that you are keeping watch over me. God, encourage me for the journey. This is my prayerful whisper. Amen.

Reflection

Invite God into this moment. What situations in your life have caused you to cry out?

Do you believe that God heard you and answered your plea?

What will sharing this experience do for someone who needs to know that God hears them?

What sacred whisper do you want to share with God today?

GOD, SOUND THE ALARM

In today's devotional moment with God, we reflect on one of many difficult moments in the life of the Prophet Jeremiah, and how his conversations with God emboldened his faith. His story illustrates to us that unwavering faith is a necessity for combating cultural conformity.

Jeremiah's entire prophetic assignment and biblical story was to voice God's displeasure, and impending judgment for the people of Judah. Every prophetic word Jeremiah spoke fell on deaf ears. To complicate matters even more, there were false prophets prophesying simultaneously, and they had mastered the art of telling the people exactly what they wanted to hear. In return, they benefited financially, maintained a premier social status, and held the people's adoration. But Jeremiah consistently warned the people that their disobedience and disregard for God would result in them being conquered and captured. He never wavered on these warnings, and as a result, he was thrown into a cistern to starve and die.

When the days that Jeremiah had prophesied about came to fruition, it was just as God had spoken. The Babylonians took the city, burned it down, and killed everyone who refused to willingly surrender. As the people were gathered and grouped for transition to captivity in Babylon, Jeremiah was unshackled and freed because the anointing of God was upon him, and even his enemies dared not touch or do him any harm for fear of God.

> "There are going to be seasons in our lives when we will have to choose faith over fear and refuse to conform."

There may have been times when we were the only person in the room that could see the walls starting to crack and cave in. People seemed oblivious to what was happening and were deaf to the prophetic voices in the group. No one listened to the potential consequences of proposed decisions and couldn't see that the benefits would be short-lived. Unfortunately, we may have kept quiet when the alarms were sounding because we wanted to avoid conflicts with our colleagues. We may have dismissed spiritual warning signs because no one else seemed to be aware of them. In truth, we went along to get along.

Jeremiah's conversation teaches us that we should always trust and believe what we hear from God. His trust in God was how he was able to refuse any conformity to a corrupt culture. God was going to devastate and destroy, and the only remedy for the people was to repent and return to God. While Jeremiah obediently offered God's solution to the people, he refused to be part of the problem and stood solo in that season. Courageous, yes. Bold, yes. Obedient, absolutely!

The takeaway for us today is that there are going to be seasons in our lives when we will have to choose faith over fear and refuse to conform. In our sacred spaces, let us pray about what we fear, and ask God to strengthen and embolden our faith and obedience. Then with a prayerful whisper ask, *God, sound the alarm.*

"When the commander of the guard found Jeremiah, he said to him, "The Lord your God decreed this disaster for this place. And now the Lord has brought it about; he has done just as he said he would. All this happened because you people sinned against the Lord and did not obey him."

Jeremiah 40:2-3

Prayer

Father God, I ask and pray that you show me the warning signs in my life. God, help me make a course correction so that I can remain faithful to your will and the truth of your Word. This is my prayerful whisper. Amen.

Reflection

Invite God into this moment. Are you ignoring warning signs in your life?

What do you think God expects you to do in unpopular situations?

What sacred whispers would you like to share with God today?

GOD, SPEAK THROUGH ME

In today's devotional moment with God, we reflect on the Apostle Paul's conversation with God. God divinely confirmed and validated his ministry and mission. Paul's story illustrates to us that we should listen to God's voice to confirm and validate us.

When Paul arrived in the city of Corinth and encountered believing Jews who had been exiled from Rome, he was excited about the possibility of his success in the city. Encouraged, Paul devoted himself to preaching and testifying to the Jews in the synagogue every sabbath. But instead of conversion and conviction, he met with opposition and expulsion. This is when Paul pivoted from the Jews to the Gentiles. Whatever the circumstances may have been, the bible records that Paul shook the dust from his clothes and refused any responsibility for their unbelief. He had faithfully preached the gospel of Jesus Christ but had failed to change the hearts and minds of his own people. Paul left the synagogue and entered the home of a worshiper of God, and when he preached the message of Jesus the Messiah, the entire household and many Corinthians believed and were baptized. This was the validation that Paul needed. God confirmed in a vision that he should preach without inhibition because He would be with him, and be his protection, provision, and peace.

> "Our prayers should be specific and ask God to make our witness worthy enough to influence other lives for Jesus."

Today we have the benefit of the Bible, and it teaches us what to say and do, and how we should do it. We have an advantage over the early disciples of the Christian faith because of our direct access to God's Word, and the opportunities afforded to us by God through Jesus Christ. However, it doesn't negate the difficulty of convincing the unbelieving heart, that salvation is made available to all through Jesus.

In our sacred spaces, we can converse with God and pray for those who still have no revelation. Our prayers should be specific and ask God to make our witness worthy enough to influence other lives for Jesus. Therefore, when we pray for our unbelieving family members, friends, and neighbors, let us include the prayerful whisper, *God, speak through me.*

"But when they opposed Paul and became abusive, he shook out his clothes in protest and said to them, "Your blood be on your own heads! I am innocent of it. From now on I will go to the Gentiles."

Acts 18:6

Prayer

Father God, give me the tenacity of the Apostle Paul to teach and preach the gospel of Jesus Christ in whatever place you send me as your disciple. This is my prayerful whisper. Amen.

Reflection

Invite God into this moment. Is there something in your life that is keeping you from ministering to unbelieving people groups? If so, can you name it?

What do you need from God to help you resolve it?

What sacred whisper would you like to share with God today?

GOD, THANK YOU FOR CALLING ME

In today's devotional moment with God, we reflect on the moment that Peter realized that he was having a conversation with God. Peter's story illustrates to us that despite our flaws we can still draw near to God.

Peter was a fisherman, and by today's standards, he would be considered a blue-collar worker. He showed up to the job every day, worked hard, and hoped to make enough wages to put food on the table, keep a roof over his head, and have sandals for his feet.

Peter along with his business partners James and John had been out all night fishing, and just as the sun was rising, they returned to the shore with empty nets. The Bible does not tell us what their state of mind was, but only that they were approached by Jesus who instructed them to get back into the boat for a redo. Following Jesus' command, they pushed away from the shore and cast their nets into the water. Immediately their nets were full of fish. The catch was so large that their boats began to sink. This was the moment that Peter realized that this man had to be God's Messiah. Peter's first instinct was to confess that he was not worthy of the miracle or catch of fish because he was a sinner. However, Jesus did not reject him, admonish him, or condemn him, but invited Peter to follow Him and become a fisher of men.

> "Jesus sees past our current issues because He knows the purpose we will fulfill tomorrow."

The conversation between Jesus and Peter has relevance for us today. Jesus knew exactly who Peter was on that day in Gennesaret. The blue-collar, hardworking, rough-edged Peter who had kneeled in a moment of confession would become responsible for building the foundation upon which today's Christian church still stands.

The central message of today's devotion is that Jesus sees past our current issues because He knows the purpose we will fulfill tomorrow. It can be challenging to leave places and people we feel comfortable and confident with, but when God calls us to follow Him, we should go willingly and without hesitation. We have to be prepared and ready in our sacred spaces to process what it means to be called to do something bigger than ourselves. Today, let us prayerfully whisper, *God, thank you for calling me.*

*When Simon Peter saw this, he fell at Jesus' knees and said,
"Go away from me, Lord; I am a sinful man!"For he and all his
companions were astonished at the catch of fish they had
taken, and so were James and John, the sons of Zebedee,
Simon's partners.*

Luke 5:8-9

Prayer

*Father God, I pray that I will be open and ready to invite you
into the difficult times when my words, attitudes, and behaviors
do not reflect who you are in my life. This is my prayerful
whisper. Amen*

Reflection

Invite God into this moment. What level of access will you give
God so that He can step into your life?

Are you functioning with the faith that allows you to follow
Jesus into your future? If not, what is holding you back?

What sacred whispers would you like to share with God today?

GOD, HELP ME TO PIVOT

In today's devotional moment with God, we reflect on Cain's decisions and how they prompted a conversation with God. Cain's story illustrates to us that God responds to our disobedience as well as our obedience but not in a good way.

The context of this conversation happened after Adam and Eve had disobeyed God, and as a consequence were evicted from the Garden of Eden. As the first humans, it was their sin that brought forth the consequence of death, and their children were not exempt. They had two sons, Cain the farmer, and Abel the shepherd. Neither of them had experienced God as their parents had in the Garden, and their knowledge of God was limited to reverence and duty.

At the appointed time of atonement, Cain presented an offering that was rejected by God, but Abel's offering was accepted. This infuriated Cain, and when God admonished him for his choice of an offering and warned him of the detrimental consequences of his sin, Cain became enraged. Cain snapped and killed his brother Abel. Then came the question from God, "What have you done?

> "Stillness helps us to focus on hearing God so that we can process our decisions and make choices that won't have detrimental consequences."

Most of us would never want to hear God ask us the question He asked Cain. This is because the question itself implies that the forthcoming consequences will be too much to bear. However, many of us have experienced successful seasons and believed that what we had achieved was because we worked hard. God was given no credit for our successes. God was not even a part of the thought process because we had assumed a haughty posture. Unfortunately, it was only in hindsight that we recognized the error of disregarding God, and sadly there were no do-overs. Yet, God allowed us to pivot, repent, and be reconciled with Him.

God had warned Cain as a way of allowing him to pivot and make a different decision, but he ignored the warning. God warns us to pivot as well, and we should listen for our benefit. This is why we must learn to be still in our sacred spaces with God. Stillness helps us to focus on hearing God so that we can process our decisions and make choices that won't have detrimental consequences.

What we learn today from Cain's conversation with God is that when our decisions and actions are being called into question, it is probably because we are operating outside of the will of God and need to pivot. Therefore, let our prayerful whisper be, *God, help me pivot.*

"The Lord said, "What have you done? Listen! Your brother's blood cries out to me from the ground. "

Genesis 4:10

Prayer

Father God, I pray that you will help me to recognize when I am operating outside of your will, and have become angry with you and others. God, I ask for your guidance to know when to pivot so that I do not fall into sin and endure detrimental consequences. This is my prayerful whisper. Amen.

Reflection

Invite God into this moment. Can you remember a time in your life when you needed to pivot to avoid detrimental consequences?

What advice or guidance can you give to someone else experiencing haughtiness and anger issues?

What sacred whispers would you like to share with God today?

GOD, THIS MISSION
IS NOT IMPOSSIBLE

In today's devotional moment with God, we reflect on the birth announcement of Jesus Christ and the conversation between God's messenger and the virgin Mary. Mary's story illustrates to us that God can do extraordinary things in the lives of ordinary people.

The divine birth announcement was made to Mary during a visit from the Lord's Angel Gabriel. As God's designated messenger, he understood that the assignment was to deliver the message accurately without any variations. The Lord's Angel Gabriel revealed that God had declared Mary highly favored and blessed among women. She would be the mother of God's only son Jesus. Mary was on the prefaces of birthing a Savior. However, her immediate mission would be to survive the scrutiny, condemnation, and a stoning for being an unwed pregnant woman in a small devout Jewish town.

> "God is continuing to speak to ordinary people and leading them to do extraordinary things."

In today's context, we would say that this was a drop-the-mic moment. If you have ever heard the expression, *the big stuff is in the small details,* then this would certainly apply to Mary's story. The insights displayed in the small details of the immaculate conception were theophanic, supernatural, and miraculous. One of the most significant insights was that God favored an unknown young woman, from a small inconsequential town, and called her blessed. God trusted Mary with His son and the salvation of humanity. To her credit, she believed God emphatically, and a Savior was born.

We must recognize that impossible missions are not a thing of the past. God is continuing to speak to ordinary people and leading them to do extraordinary things. It's amazing when we hear of an extraordinary event on the news or in a podcast. We might find ourselves asking what we would have done in an emergent situation, and whether we were courageous enough to act heroically. Mary could have easily ignored the message and messenger, but it would not have changed God's plan for her life. She was chosen for seemingly an impossible mission, but when God is with us, the impossible becomes possible.

As we enter into our sacred spaces with God, let us remember that He has a divine plan and purpose for each of us. Therefore, let us be prepared to process and pray about situations and assignments that may seem impossible, and know that God is listening to our prayerful whispers when we ask, *God, make this mission possible.*

"I am the Lord's servant," Mary answered. "May your word to me be fulfilled."Then the angel left her.

Luke 1:38

Prayer

Father God, I pray that you will allow me to discern when it's your messenger speaking to me so that I will continue to be intentional in doing your will. God, I am your servant, and I pray your word will be fulfilled in my life. This is my prayerful whisper. Amen.

Reflection

Invite God into this moment. What message has God sent to you by a messenger and you're ignoring it?

What do you need to hear from God to have the confidence to move forward?

What sacred whisper would you like to share with God today?

GOD, YOUR SERVANT IS LISTENING

In today's devotional moment with God, we reflect on the conversation between God and the boy Samuel. Samuel's story illustrates to us that God should be our priority.

Samuel was the young protégé of the Prophet Eli. He had come to be in Eli's care because of his mother Hannah. She had prayed for a child and promised God that if he blessed her, she would return the child to Him. The Bible records that during this period, the prophets did not receive many visions. Nonetheless, Samuel was prepared for prophetic service and learned to serve and keep God's covenants under the tutelage of Eli.

Eli had two sons, Hophni and Phinehas but they were corrupt. They stole the people's offerings, took sacrifices designated for God, engaged in adulterous behavior, and disregarded the rebuke of their father Eli.

The first time Samuel heard God call his name, he did not realize it was God. Three times God called Samuel before Eli instructed him to listen because God was speaking. Then Samuel received a *rare* prophetic word. God appointed him as the new prophet of Israel because Eli and all of his descendants would be destroyed. Although he loved Eli, God was his priority.

"When we establish our priorities and expectations for our lives, serving God should be at the top of our list."

Samuel's transition to prophetic ministry was unusual at best. Although his life had been committed to the service of God before his birth, he had not refused to serve God, nor had he planned to renege on his mother's promise to God. This was because Samuel could not conceive of his life without God. God was the one relationship that he desired and trusted most, and not because of power or position but because of a covenant made on his behalf before his existence. Samuel knew that God kept His promises and honored His covenants, and no other relationship could compare or compete. This is why God would be his priority, and why God should be our priority.

Therefore, when we establish our priorities and expectations for our lives, serving God should be at the top of our list. When we are making our prayers and petitions known to God in our sacred spaces, we should listen for God and include the prayerful whisper, *God, your servant is listening.*

*The Lord came and stood there, calling as at the other times,
"Samuel! Samuel!"
Then Samuel said, "Speak, for your servant is
listening."*

1 Samuel 3:10

Prayer

*Father God, I pray that I am spiritually ready for the revelation
you have for my life. God, help me to be committed and faithful
to serve you daily. This is my prayerful whisper. Amen.*

Reflection

Invite God into this moment. Do you recognize God's voice in
your own life?

What is God calling you to do?

What sacred whispers would you like to share with God today?

GOD, WE NEED YOU AND NOT A SIGN

In today's devotional moment with God, we reflect on Jesus' message and conversation with the crowd in the midst of a miraculous moment. Jesus' story illustrates to us that God is continuing to perform miracles, and there is no need for a sign from heaven.

The crowd was a mixed group of people. Among them were the disciples, religious leaders, the possessed, and the sick. Jesus was teaching and casting out demons when some members of the crowd demanded a sign from heaven. Immediately He admonished them because they challenged what they had witnessed with their own eyes. The issue was not with the miracle but with the Messiah. Jesus did not have the appearance of their Messiah and was too natural and not majestic enough. Even though Jesus had the Word of God on His lips, and the power of God in His hands, the people would not believe.

> "In our sacred spaces with God, we should look for clarity and not signs."

This account of one of the many miracles of Jesus is per-plexing for us today. This is because the crowd was challenging their own eyewitness of miracles. In its historical context, Jews believed that any miracle performed at the command of God had to be confirmed with a sign. Unfortunately, the reason they wanted Jesus to give them a sign was that their traditions would not allow them to confirm the truth of His identity.

If we are to be honest, we may have had moments in our own lives when we have asked God for a sign. This may be particularly true when our prayers have gone unanswered for some time, or when we had a tough decision to make and wanted to be sure that God had answered.

The lesson for us today is that Jesus miraculously handled the needs of the people then, and miraculously handles our needs now. In our sacred spaces with God, we should look for clarity and not signs. When we need confirmation, let us go to God with the prayerful whisper, *God, we need you and not a sign.*

"As the crowds increased, Jesus said, "This is a wicked gener-
ation. It asks for a sign, but none will be given it except the sign
of Jonah. "

Luke 11:29

Prayer

Father God, I pray that you will help me to recognize your
wonder-working power, and not doubt that you can do anything.
God, increase the capacity of my faith so that I am able to ex-
perience you more fully. This is my prayerful whisper. Amen.

Reflection

Invite God into this moment. What would help you be more
aware of God's presence in your life?

Have there been times when you didn't recognize God's miraculous interventions? What insights do you have from these
experiences?

What sacred whisper would you like to share with God today?

GOD, THERE'S NO NEED TO SEARCH FOR YOU

In today's devotional moment with God, we reflect on the conversation between God and the Prophet Elijah. Elijah's story illustrates to us that God is always with us.

God asked, 'What are you doing here, Elijah? Here, was a reference to the cave on Mount Horeb. For forty days, Elijah had traveled the wilderness to meet God on His mountain. Exhausted and distraught, Elijah recalled every detail of the battle on Mount Carmel with the four hundred and fifty false prophets of Baal and Jezebel. Each time God asked him, he repeated his answer. The problem with Elijah's answer was that he kept repeating the details of the battle as if God was not there. God was there! And Elijah endured nothing alone.

> "Everything we endured in this life was a shared experience with God. This is because God is omnipresent and has never missed a moment of our life."

If Elijah's story resonates with us, it is because we too have tried to make sense of difficult situations in our lives. We have probably had moments when we have questioned God as to why any of it was necessary. The truth is everything we have endured in this life was a shared experience with God. This is because God is omnipresent and has never missed a moment of our life. We don't need to run to a mountain or to a church to meet or be present with God. We can invite Him into our lives and expect that He will remain. Our sacred spaces provide us with the safety to work through life challenges and get all of our questions, concerns, and prayers answered. Then, with prayerful whispers confirm, *God, there's no need to search for you.*

There *he went into a cave and spent the night. And the word of the Lord came to him: "What are you doing here, Elijah?" He replied, "I have been very zealous for the Lord God Almighty. The Israelites have rejected your covenant, torn down your altars, and put your prophets to death with the sword. I am the only one left, and now they are trying to kill me too."*

1 Kings 19:9-10.

Prayer

Father God, let me have the assurance of your nearness. God, teach me to trust you and know that you will never leave me or abandon me. This is my prayerful whisper. Amen.

Reflection

Invite God into this moment. What do you need to be assured that God is present with you in every moment of your life?

Can you recall times in your life when you were doubtful about whether God was near?

What sacred whisper would you like to share with God today?

GOD, REPLENISH MY EMPTINESS

In today's devotional moment with God, we reflect on the story of Naomi, and the conversations that occurred because of her faith in God. Naomi's story illustrates to us that our faith in God can be influential to others. Although the conversations were between Naomi, Ruth, and Boaz, they were meant for God to hear. This is because the content of these conversations was about covenant-keeping as the people of God.

The woman Naomi was a widow who had been living in the land of Moab because of a great famine in Bethlehem. When her husband and sons died, Naomi instructed her two daughters-in-law to return to their own people, so that she could return to hers. Orpha left Naomi, but Ruth refused to leave her to fend for herself. In an effort to convince Naomi of her commitment, she vowed to accept her people and God as her own. When they arrived in Bethlehem, Naomi was lauded and welcomed by her people, but life had not been kind, and she had become bitter. However, Ruth kept her word and remained dutifully at Naomi's side. Naomi navigated every step of Ruth's new life in this new community of people, and her obedience made her the source of God's provision for the good that was to come into their lives.

> "Our sacred spaces with God are where we talk through painful seasons so that bitterness does not become blinding to restorative blessings."

We may have had seasons when life was unkind to us. During these seasons we retreated into our feelings and refused the help of our support systems. We allowed our bitterness to become pervasive and were spiritually blind to the provisions of God. This was possibly Naomi's posture and predicament when she entered the gates of Bethlehem empty-handed, and without a male heir to claim the family's inheritance. In all of her bitterness, Naomi had failed to recognize that Ruth was God's provision and plan for her future. This is why it is important that we work through grief and loss and not allow bitterness to blind us to the blessings of God.

Our sacred spaces with God are where we talk through painful seasons so that bitterness does not become blinding to restorative blessings. Then, ask God with a repentant heart and in a prayerful whisper, *God, replenish my emptiness.*

"So Boaz took Ruth, and she became his wife. When he made love to her, the Lord enabled her to conceive, and she gave birth to a son. The woman said to Naomi: "Praise be to the Lord, who this day has not left you without a guardian-redeemer. May he become famous throughout Israel!"

Ruth 4:13-14

Prayer

Father God, I pray that you will release me from all anger and bitterness that hinders me from welcoming both change and provision into my life. God, open my heart and mind to you so that I don't fall away when I'm empty. This is my prayerful whisper. Amen

Reflection

Invite God into this moment. Are you struggling with bitterness in areas of your life?

What can you learn from Naomi's story that will encourage you for this season?

What sacred whisper would you like to share with God today?

GOD, THANK YOU FOR PERFECTING THE JESUS IN ME

In today's devotional moment with God, we reflect on the Sermon on the Mount, and the conversation that Jesus directed to the crowds gathered. Jesus' story illustrates to us that although difficult, God expects us to love one another.

Noticing that the crowds had not dissipated and had continued to follow Him throughout the region of the Jordan, Jesus positioned himself on top of a mount near the Lake of Gennesaret. There He sat down and taught what has become the greatest master class of modern Christianity. With the full attention of His disciples and the crowds, Jesus skillfully unpacked the laws of Moses, but with a revision to the decree of retribution. His disciples were to handle the Mosaic Law within the context of love instead of retribution. This meant that they would not be judges or adjudicators, retaliatory or revengers, but servants to the people. They were expected to love without exception and embrace human imperfection with compassion. Jesus expected His disciples to love like God.

> "Righteous living requires a relationship with Jesus that conforms to kingdom standards, and not to the standards or mandates of the world."

Today there are several teachings of Jesus that we as His disciples may continue to wrestle with. This is because of the selfless sacrifice that is expected of us. We are expected to turn the other cheek and love our neighbor as ourselves. We are expected to care for the sick, visit the imprisoned, feed the hungry, clothe the naked, and shelter the homeless, and do it all without complaint or applause. We are expected to respond like this because this was Jesus' example. Yet, we have to be careful and conscious that the message of Jesus' ministry does not become muddled in its meaning. The message is that righteous living requires a relationship with Jesus that conforms to kingdom standards, and not to the standards or mandates of the world.

Jesus never expected perfection from imperfect people. But He does expect His followers to imitate Him by responding with love and compassion, and not condemnation. Therefore, in our sacred spaces and devotional time with God, let us prayerfully whisper, *God, thank you for perfecting the Jesus in me.*

"Now when Jesus saw the crowds, he went up on a mountainside and sat down. His disciples came to him, and he began to teach them."

Matthew 5:1-2

Prayer

Father God, I pray that you will perfect the right spirit in me to serve your people with uninhibited compassion and love. This is my prayerful whisper. Amen.

Reflection

Invite God into this moment. What can you do to imitate Jesus in your life as a faithful follower and committed disciple?

What sacred whisper would you like to share with God today?

GOD, BLESS ME

In today's devotional moment with God, we return to a difficult conversation between the Prophet Nathan and King David. David's story illustrates to us that we should not take God's grace for granted.

David had been chosen by God as a young boy to succeed Saul as the anointed king of Israel. Once David ascended to king, God blessed him. A blessed David united the Israelite kingdoms and fortified their territories and increased their wealth. A blessed David worshiped before the people without inhibition and was legendary because God was with him. Songs were sung about his victories and stories were told about his prowess and power. In the eyes of the people, the blessed David was invincible. This was until David committed a sin so deplorable, that God was greatly offended. David was blessed but he could not conceal his sin from the ever-watchful eyes of God.

During his time, it was customary for the Prophet or people to seek his counsel for disputes, judgments, and losses. One day, the Prophet Nathan told David a story of a poor man who lost his only asset which was one lamb. A wealthy man had ordered his servants to slaughter this lamb to satisfy the needs of a traveler because he didn't want to take from his wealth or possessions. This left the poor man with no assets. The King was infuriated and demanded retribution up to four times the loss. Then, the Prophet Nathan named David as the culprit and described the consequences of his sin. David immediately repented but the atonement would not be his life, but the life of the child who was conceived by his adultery.

> "We must be intentional in our efforts to please God with our obedience and righteous living."

As scandalous as this story is for us today, at some level, we are all capable of committing sins so deplorable that they offend God. Yes, Jesus died on the cross to redeem us from eternal condemnation, and although it is enough to be saved by grace, we must still be intentional in a holy relationship with God. We must be intentional in our efforts to please God with our obedience and righteous living. We must be intentional in our efforts to worship God daily, and not just with our words but with our witness. We cannot take God's grace for granted like King David. This is why our daily intention should be to connect with God in our sacred spaces so that we can examine ourselves, repent, and ask for forgiveness. As we pray, let our repentant heart echo the prayerful whisper, *God, bless me.*

"David burned with anger against the man and said to Nathan, "As surely as the Lord lives, the man who did this must die! He must pay for that lamb four times over because he did such a thing and had no pity."Then Nathan said to David, "You are the man!"

2 Samuel 12:5-7

Prayer

Father God, I pray to be more aware of the pricelessness of your grace, and not take your grace for granted. God, guide me to be more intentional in my relationship with you so that you are pleased with my obedience and service. This is my prayerful whisper. Amen.

Reflection

Invite God into this moment. Can you recall a time in your life when you took God's grace for granted?

What advice would you give to a Christian struggling with issues of selfishness and sinfulness?

What sacred whisper would you like to share with God today?

GOD, HELP ME TO BLINDLY BELIEVE

In today's devotional moment with God, we reflect on Abram's story and the conversation in which he heard God promise him a son. Abram's story illustrates to us that whatever God has promised we should believe.

The promise of an heir occurs as a part of a sequence of divine events. With only 318 men from among his servants, Abram rescued his relative Lot and recovered all of his possessions from the skilled armies of Sodom. With armies surrounding him, Abram rejected an alliance with the King of Sodom to maintain his allegiance solely with God. With tensions rising, Abram is visited by Melchizedek who is described in the bible as the Priest of the Highest God. This final brief theophanic encounter was to affirm God's covenant with him. Then, God spoke to him in a vision. Abram could not have imagined this moment, because God spoke that he would have a son of his bloodline. His descendants would solidify his name, his legacy would continue into perpetuity, and their numbers would be greater than the stars. Abram didn't ask God when this would happen because he blindly believed God.

> "The further we are from the familiar comforts and the influences of family and friends, the more time we will have to converse and figure life out with God."

Rescues, battles, victories, and covenant promises all happened for the benefit of Abram because he blindly believed in God. Whenever we consider Abram, and who he was historically, it is not surprising that he responded to God in this way. After all, Abram had left his father's house and all of his family to follow God. In fact, Abram never asked God to prove anything to him and believed God anyway. The further Abram was away from home the more God spoke with him. The further we are from the familiar comforts and the influences of family and friends, the more time we will have to converse and figure life out with God.

When we spend time with God in our sacred spaces, the Holy Spirit helps us to discern what doesn't align with God's will, so that we can be free of fear and blindly believe. For this reason, let us process our fears as well as our faith, and with a prayerful whisper ask, *God, help me to blindly believe.*

*"Abram believed the Lord, and he credited it to him as
righteousness."*

Genesis 15:6

Prayer

*Father God, I ask that you help me to grow into a believer who
has the faith to blindly believe and follow you into new territory.
This is my prayerful whisper. Amen.*

Reflection

Invite God into this moment. What are you afraid of hearing
from God?

What will it take for you to have blind faith like Abram?

What sacred whisper would you like to share with God today?

GOD, JUST SAY THE WORD

In today's devotional moment with God, we reflect on the conversation between Jesus and the Centurion who pursued Him for a miracle. The Centurion's story illustrates to us that our faith will get us an audience with Jesus.

The Centurion was a commander in the Roman army with at least one hundred soldiers under his authority. He was a man of high standing, but he knew he would not receive any preferential treatment from Jesus. With this in mind, the Centurion joined the crowds and walked amongst them because he needed a miracle. Before Jesus ever entered a community, the news of the miracles he had performed were known, and people either followed to see the miracles for themselves or to be healed. Every person in the crowd who had followed Jesus to Capernaum was hopeful to be either a witness or a recipient.

With the boldness of a Roman army commander, the Centurion stepped out of the crowd and asked Jesus to heal his servant who lay paralyzed, sick, and suffering. The faith of this Centurion was so great that he confessed that he was not worthy to have Jesus' come into his home. However, he asked Jesus to speak the words because he believed that this would heal his servant. Honoring his request, Jesus spoke the words of healing, and the life of the Centurion's servant was miraculously restored.

> "Let us take our cues from the Centurion and go directly to Jesus and ask for whatever we need for our lives to be restored, redeemed, and renewed."

We can probably all recall a time when our lives were vastly different than they are today. In those seasons, we may have refused to invite Jesus into our lives because we believed we weren't worthy. Our lifestyles weren't idyllic for a Christian, and we assumed that God was offended and would never respond to our prayers. Whatever we may have believed, it was a lie. This erroneous perspective of God excluded the grace, mercy, and forgiveness made available to us by the atoning sacrifice of Jesus.

Today, let us take our cues from the Centurion and go directly to Jesus and ask for whatever we need for our lives to be restored, redeemed, and renewed. In our sacred spaces, we can talk with God and experience Him for ourselves as He intended, and ask with a prayerful whisper, *God, just say the word.*

"The centurion replied, "Lord, I do not deserve to have you come under my roof. But just say the word, and my servant will be healed."

Matthew 8:8

Prayer

Father God, I pray that I will never block your access to my life regardless of what it looks like. God, I know that I am not worthy of you, but I am thankful for the grace and mercy you have given me in love. This is my prayerful whisper. Amen.

Reflection

Invite God into this moment. Is there something that you need to do right now so that you feel comfortable inviting Jesus into your personal life and sacred spaces?

What sacred whisper would you like to share with God today?

GOD, TAKE AWAY DOUBT

In today's devotional moment with God, we reflect on Jesus' conversation with The Apostles as he walked on the water towards them. The Apostles' story illustrates to us that miracles require faith. Jesus' Apostles continued to struggle with their faith, especially when He was not physically present with them. The Apostles had boarded a boat to cross over to the other side of the lake at Jesus' request. As the crowds dispersed, Jesus retreated to the mountain alone and stayed until the early morning hours. In His descent, He noticed that the boat swayed because of the high winds and waves. Jesus stepped onto the water and walked across it to His Apostles. Although they were waiting for Jesus, they became frightened when they saw Him on the water near the boat. To calm their fears, Jesus confirmed His identity and revealed His deity. At Peter's request, Jesus invited him to step onto the water and into a miraculous moment. But Peter's faith was not substantial enough to keep him from sinking.

We can stop wrestling with faith when we truly believe in the omnipotence of God.

As Christians, we continue to wrestle with faith, fear, and doubt. This is because we have no revelation or understanding of the supernatural power of God in a natural situation, or how divine interventions solve our problems and predicaments. However, we can stop wrestling with faith when we truly believe in the omnipotence of God. The Apostles had been witnesses to numerous miracles, but they were still unprepared to see the supernatural in the natural world.

Today's devotional is an opportunity to reflect on our preparation for miraculous moments. We should desire to be ready when Jesus asks us to trust Him and step into a supernatural situation. In our sacred spaces, we can process fear and doubt and God's omnipotence. Then when we pray for Jesus to show up and handle the high winds and waves that cause turbulence in our lives, we will be ready. Therefore, let us prayerfully whisper, *God, take away the doubt.*

Immediately Jesus reached out his hand and caught him. "You of little faith," he said, "why did you doubt?"

Matthew 14:31

Prayer

Father God, as a seasoned, developing, or new believer of the Christian faith, I pray that you will help me to be prepared for miraculous moments. This is my prayerful whisper. Amen.

Reflection

Invite God into this moment. Ask yourself, am I still struggling with doubt in my relationship with God?

What has to change in your relationship with God to decrease your doubt and fear?

What sacred whisper would you like to share with God today?

GOD, HELP ME FULFILL MY DIVINE ASSIGNMENT

In today's devotional moment with God, we reflect on the story of the 12-year-old Jesus, and the conversation between Him and His earthly parents, Joseph and Mary. Jesus' parent's story illustrates to us the commitment we should have to our divine assignments.

The Gospel of Luke records a rare look at the early life of a young Jesus. The boy Jesus had decided to stay in Jerusalem once the annual celebration of the *Feast of Passover* had concluded. He stayed in the city without Joseph and Mary's knowledge. When they realized that Jesus was missing, they headed back to Jerusalem to search for Him. Three days had passed before they found Jesus sitting in the temple courts listening to the teachers and asking and answering questions. With the heightened concern of a mother, Mary asked Jesus why He had created worry for them and stayed in the city without their knowledge. The answer Jesus gave seems dismissive at first glance, but we need to understand that even at an early age Jesus was focused on His divine assignment. However, what is also apparent is the commitment Joseph and Mary had to fulfill their own divine assignment.

> "Our parenting assignment has a bigger purpose
> than we can see at the moment. In our sacred spaces,
> we should ask God for the support we need as parents
> to guide our children in fulfilling their purpose."

For those of us who are parents or caregivers, we understand the enormous stress of losing sight of our children in a public place like a park, grocery store, or shopping center. Although we may have talked with and taught our children about stranger danger, and not walking away from us in public places, we know that there are no guarantees with their limited attention spans. The reality is that our children have their own free will, and it can override our efforts at any given moment.

In the context of today's devotional, no one should question why Joseph and Mary would have been worried about Jesus. Jesus was indeed God in the flesh, but He was also their child. They had a divine assignment, and it was to care for Jesus. More importantly, they understood that their parenting assignment had a bigger purpose.

This is what we need to take away from Joseph and Mary, and that is that our parenting assignment has a bigger purpose than we can see at the moment. In our sacred spaces, we should ask God for the support we need as parents to guide our children in fulfilling their purpose, and prayerfully whisper, *God, help me fulfill my divine assignment.*

"Why were you searching for me?" he asked. "Didn't you know I had to be in my Father's house?"But they did not under-stand what he was saying to them."

Luke 2:49-50

Prayer

Father God, I pray that you will give me the grace and wisdom to parent the children in my life the way that you have parented me. God, may I always be mindful that parenting is a God-given assignment with a greater purpose. This is my prayerful whisper. Amen.

Reflection

Invite God into this moment. Have you prayed and asked God to help you with the parenting assignment?

Do you have some unresolved issues with how you were parented, and worry that these issues may impact your parenting style? If so, prayerfully decide how you can create a plan to unpack these issues spiritually and emotionally.

What sacred whisper would you like to share with God today?

GOD, LIGHTEN THE LOAD

In today's devotional moment with God, we reflect on the wilderness experience of Moses and the Israelites after they fled slavery in Egypt. Moses' story illustrates to us that God does not expect us to bear burdens alone.

The context of this conversation between God and Moses happened after God rained down a consuming fire on the outskirts of the camp of the Israelites. God was responding to their constant complaints. When the people cried out to Moses because of the fire, he petitioned God for mercy and the fire ceased, but the complaints did not. By the time Moses expressed his fatigue and frustration, God had responded to their previous complaints by delivering them from slavery and providing manna for bread. As the complaints continued, God became increasingly angered, and Moses was exhausted with the insatiable demands of the people. To end his exasperation, Moses asked God to relieve him of the burden of six hundred thousand men within the Israelite camp. At the direction of God, he gathered seventy men who were Elders of Israel and assigned them to care for the people. Each Elder received a small portion of the anointing that God had given to Moses. Moses was relieved of bearing the full burden alone.

> "When we are overwhelmed with life, then we should take a much needed moment with God in our sacred spaces and process solutions with Him."

Moses' moment of conversation and self-disclosure could not have been easy. This is because he was complaining to God about the Israelites' constant complaints. They wanted too much from him, and regardless of how he tried to meet their needs, they were buckets with holes in them.

We all have certain people in our own lives who overwhelm us with their constant demands for our time and attention. Yet, every effort we make to nurture these relationships is never enough. Moses needed a moment with God. He needed a moment for God to hear that the divine assignment was no longer manageable for him, and he was distressed and discouraged with life. Moses' conversation should serve as a reminder that God is the source of our solutions.

When we are overwhelmed with life, then we should take a much-needed moment with God in our sacred spaces and process solutions with Him. This is why conversations with God matter, and because they do, we can go with the prayerful whisper, *God, lighten my load.*

*"The Lord said to Moses: "Bring me seventy of Israel's elders
who are known to you as leaders and officials among the
people. Have them come to the tent of the meeting, that they
may stand there with you.I will come down and speak with you
there, and I will take some of the power of the Spirit that is on
you and put it on them. They will share the burden of the
people with you so that you will not have to carry it alone."*

Numbers 11:16-17

Prayer

*Father God, teach me how to come to you first with the things
in my life that overwhelm and burden me. God, help me to
hear your plans and solutions for my life. This is my prayerful
whisper. Amen.*

Reflection

Invite God into this moment. What is overwhelming you that
you need to go to God for a solution?

When was the last time that you aired your list of complaints?

What sacred whisper would you like to share with God today?

GOD, I'M THANKFUL YOU KNOW MY NAME

In today's devotional moment with God, we reflect on the conversation between God and Saul after he heard the Lord call him by name. Saul's story illustrates to us that when God calls our name, we must answer the call.

Saul had been on a personal crusade to persecute Christians in Jerusalem. He had even traveled throughout Samaria and Judea searching for any followers of Jesus to imprison. Equipped with letters from the church granting him permission to persecute, Saul traveled toward Damascus in pursuit of the followers of the Way. On the road to Damascus, Saul encountered a theophany. With unexpected bursts of lights descending from heaven and engulfing him, he fell to the ground. Then a voice called out to him twice by name. In a posture of submission, Saul asked who it was that was speaking to him, and Jesus answered that it was the One whom he was persecuting.

> "As Christians, we should desire to hear God call our name, not because we are destroyers, but because we are builders of the faith and are obedient servants."

At this moment in Saul's life, he believed that the followers of Jesus were blasphemers and that their Christian ideology was endangering the faith. From Saul's perspective, Jesus' faithful followers would cause a schism, and this would be detrimental to the people of God. This is why Saul had taken it as his personal mission to preserve the faith and protect the people. However, it was Saul's love of God that would make him a fervent Apostle of Jesus. Unbeknownst to Saul, his evangelistic ministry for the Christian church would become historic. When Jesus called Saul, He was converting Him to Paul, and his new convictions would change his course for Christ.

As Christians, we should desire to hear God call our name because we are faithful servants. In our sacred spaces, we can process our flawed perceptions and listen for the voice of God in our own lives. God has both a ministry and mission for us but we must prepare for our Damascus Road. Then with a prayerful whisper affirm, *God, I'm thankful you know my name.*

"He fell to the ground and heard a voice say to him, "Saul, Saul, why do you persecute me?" "Who are you, Lord?" Saul asked. "I am Jesus, whom you are persecuting," he replied. "

Acts 9:4-5

Prayer

Father God, help me to recognize your voice as a guiding light in my life. God, I pray that I will be ready to encounter you on my own Damascus Road experience and shift as needed to serve you. This is my prayerful whisper. Amen.

Reflection

Invite God into this moment. Ask God how you can be more intentional in hearing His voice in your life.

What choices have you made in your life as it relates to your relationship with God?

What sacred whisper would you like to share with God today?

ACKNOWLEDGMENTS

In brevity, there aren't enough words of thanks that can convey my gratitude and appreciation for the tremendous support of the following people. You have all been my rock! Your inspiration and daily encouragement helped to make this devotional possible.

Ron, you are the love of my life and my forever partner. Thank you for your unwavering support, love, encouragement, prayers, and the space and time to write. Most importantly, thank you for believing in me!

Christopher, Bryan, and Demetria – my beautiful children, you are all amazing people who do amazing things in your respective lives. Your mommy is proud and loves you all more than words can express.

Rev. Dr. Robert C. Jones, Jr., thank you for being my sounding board and listening ear. I can never repay you for the support and time given to processing theology and the exegesis of scripture. Your encouragement has been immeasurable. You are an awesome friend and an amazing mentor.

Rev. Roxanne Cardenas Bryant, thank you for being available to provide good counsel, support, and sisterly wisdom. And ten thousand thanks for your contribution to the back cover! My sister in ministry, you are amazing!

Mia Little, Little Designs Creative Studio, Chicago, IL. You have done it again! You have captured my vision for this book cover, and it is beautiful. Thank you for listening and making the vision happen.

Chanel Norman Moore, Chanel Production, Photography & Video Services, Raleigh, NC. Thank you for capturing the light embodied in me.

A Fresh Wind Publishing. To my Publisher Marcie Stowers-Wilson, thank you for your unwavering support, encouragement, prayers, countless hours of edits, and guidance through this project. This would have been so much more difficult without you. Much love to you always!

God, may all glory, honor, and praise be given to you, this is my prayerful whisper. Amen.

ABOUT THE AUTHOR

Reverend Linda S. Carter has been actively engaged in transformative ministry since she accepted her call in 1998. Ordained by the American Baptist Churches of the USA in 2004, she is continuing to create opportunities for believers and seekers alike to hear and have access to the Word of God.

A native of the Midwest, Carter earned her Bachelor of Science Degree from Southern Illinois University at Edwardsville and her Master of Divinity from Northern Theological Seminary. Before retiring from full-time employment, she served as an endorsed Chaplain in healthcare and hospice and held various ministry leadership positions within the local church.

Carter's continuing agenda is to serve as a vessel for God to transform lives through the profoundness of His Word. She utilizes a charismatic and candid approach to connect with people in denominational, traditional, and non-traditional settings to meet the moment, and the mission to make an impact and imprint for Christ Jesus.

Carter is a published author and released her first book entitled *The Small Fine Print: God's Plan for Your Vision* in 2021, and the companion workbook of the same title in 2022. Her new book, *Sacred Whispers: 90-Day Devotional for God's Ears Only* is slated for release in the Fall of 2023.

Carter currently resides in North Carolina and when she is not writing, preaching, or teaching, she enjoys spending time with her family.

www.lindascarter.com

www.ingramcontent.com/pod-product-compliance
Lightning Source LLC
Chambersburg PA
CBHW071142130626
46553CB00004B/1492